# The Role of Foreign Financial Assistance to Thailand in the 1980s

The papers in this volume are edited versions of papers presented at an ad hoc seminar on "The Role of Foreign Aid to Thailand in the 1980s" organized and chaired by Dr. W. David Maxwell, Dean of the College of Liberal Arts of Texas A&M University, for the Southeast Asia Development Advisory Group (SEADAG) of The Asia Society, New York, in cooperation with the Faculty of Economics of Thammasat University and the United Nations Asian Institute for Economic Development and Planning, Bangkok. The seminar was held at the Rincome Hotel, Chieng Mai, Thailand, June 20-22, 1974.

The Asia Society, a nonprofit educational institution, was founded in 1956 to enhance American understanding of Asia and Asians and to stimulate meaningful intellectual exchange across the Pacific. Within this framework, SEADAG, which is funded by the United States Agency for International Development, seeks to promote and facilitate communication and collaboration among Asian and American scholars and policymakers concerned with development in Southeast Asia.

# The Role of Foreign Financial Assistance to Thailand in the 1980s

Edited by

**W. Lee Baldwin**
Dartmouth College

**W. David Maxwell**
Texas A&M University

**Lexington Books**
D.C. Heath and Company
Lexington, Massachusetts
Toronto London

**Library of Congress Cataloging in Publication Data**

Main entry under title:

The role of foreign financial assistance to Thailand in the 1980s.

Presented at a Southeast Asia Development Advisory Group seminar held June 20-22, 1974, in Chieng Mai, Thailand.
1. Economic assistance in Thailand—Congresses. I. Baldwin, William Lee. II. Maxwell, W. David, 1926- III. Southeast Asia Development Advisory Group.
HC497.S5R64 309.2'23'09 75-18563
ISBN 0-669-00140-6



Published simultaneously in Canada.

Printed in the United States of America.

International Standard Book Number: 0-669-00140-6

Library of Congress Catalog Card Number: 75-18563

# Contents

# List of Figures

## List of Tables

# Preface

During the period June 20-22, 1974, The Asia Society, New York City, sponsored a Southeast Asia Development Advisory Group (SEADAG) ad hoc seminar at Chieng Mai, Thailand. It was a unique seminar in a number of respects. The Seminar itself was held in cooperation with the Faculty of Economics of Thammasat University and the U.N. Asian Institute for Economic Development and Planning. As this feature alone might suggest, the participatory base from which decisions were made concerning the Seminar—its participants, its topics, its *modus operandum*, even its logistics—was broader and more influenced by the host country participants than one might expect. Drs. Maxwell, Vinyu, and Narongchai worked together to plan and stage the Seminar, supported at every turn by the effective cooperation of the staff of The Asia Society.

As a result, the Seminar was essentially a Thai affair, by common agreement. Those invited to submit papers and the other participants were either Thais or foreigners with considerable experience and familiarity with Thailand. Both groups comprising the whole shared a sincere concern for, and interest in, the economic future of Thailand. Thus, despite its title, the Seminar was actually a gathering of Thais and their close professional foreign peers and colleagues to explore a particular aspect of the economic future of Thailand, rather than a gathering of foreign experts for the purpose of advising the Thais. What was sought, essentially, was a predominantly Thai view on matters of common concern. As the papers and discussion comprising this volume attest, this objective was attained to an extent perhaps unparalleled in the recent history of Thai relations with foreign advisors, aid administrators, and scholars.

Dr. Puey Ungphakorn was the intellectual linchpin of the aggregation. Head of the Prime Minister's Council of Economic Advisors, former Governor of the Bank of Thailand, former Dean of the Faculty of Economics of Thammasat University and now Thammasat's Rector, recipient of the Magsaysay Award, and past or present holder of other positions of honor and responsibility, Dr. Puey is a man of eminence in Thai intellectual, academic, financial, and governmental circles—circles not so clearly demarcated as is true in some of the "more highly developed" nations. That he was to be a participant was a fact that was early established and shamelessly used (at least, by the Chairman) to secure able participants from Thai universities and agencies, international agencies, and the U.S. Operations Mission to Thailand.

Thus by this strategem and others, it was possible to gather together a distinguished group of knowledgeable people from the various fields of activity in which Dr. Puey has made such a deep imprint—a group at almost immediate ease because of past or present associations, many of which involved Dr. Puey, directly or indirectly.

As the discussion reflects, many of the questions not directed to the authors were directed to Dr. Snoh Unakul, Director of the National Economic and Social Development Board (NESDB), and he played a coordinate role with Dr. Puey in setting the stage for the Seminar—due not only to the crucial role of the NESDB in economic planning, but also to the esteem in which he, personally, is held by the participants. While space does not permit remarks even this scanty concerning the remaining participants, suffice it to say that our assertion that it was a distinguished assemblage is attested by the backgrounds and current positions of the participants, as well as by the papers and discussion presented herein.

The Seminar was also singular in terms of the general mood that prevailed. It was held at a time when the spirit of the October (1973) uprising was still strong, and these very able and influential Thais were, for the most part, highly optimistic about the prospects of significant reform and an acceleration of social progress. And they felt free to speak openly of their aspirations and their past frustrations. An earlier time would have made events too fresh to be placed in perspective. Now, some ten months later, the euphoria is greatly diminished, and the difficulties of converting into reality the promises of a "revolution" that did not drastically change the locus of economic and political power are evident. Thus this seminar is important in coming at a time when the Thai participants "opened up" and made evident what they hoped for their country and would want in the way of financial assistance from abroad.

In a more long-run sense, the papers and discussion had a timeliness they still possess. As the record of economic growth in Thailand indicates, this nation has the potential of crossing the line into the ranks of the more highly developed nations of Asia, such as Japan and Singapore. While financial aid can be of only small magnitude relative to the more basic economic variables that will determine this country's future, such assistance—wisely deployed—could be crucial to the outcome. Implicitly, this raises a fundamental question concerning financial aid policy. While project-directed aid is often justified in terms of expected productivity, the recipient's eligibility for financial assistance may instead be determined on the basis of the country's overall immediate need, as reflected in such measures as per capita income. Thus the "reward" for approaching the threshold is decreased eligibility for the assistance that could be crucial in passing beyond it. Short-run humanitarianism may well be, in a longer and more important context, not only uneconomic but also inhumane.

This volume was compiled and edited by the Seminar rapporteur and its chairman. We wish to acknowledge our indebtedness to The Asia Society for its material support and for the encouragement and helpful suggestions of its staff, particularly Charles McVicker and Robert Bordonaro. We are also grateful for the patience and tolerance of the authors of the papers reproduced herein. Our unmerciful hounding was met—even on the part of the non-Thai authors—by the unfailing good humor so characteristic of the Thais. This in itself may be some small indication of how greatly life in the West could be improved by cultural importation from this remarkable society.

Last, but not least, we wish to thank Mrs. Peggy Lauer for an intelligent typing of the final manuscript and Khun Valairat Kuslasayanon for her assistance with the various materials processed in Bangkok. Their conscientious and thoughtful work lighten the customary responsibility that we hereby acknowlege.

# List of Participants and Observers: SEADAG Ad Hoc Seminar on Foreign Aid to Thailand in the 1980s.

## Participants

Amara Raksasataya, Dean
School of Public Administration
National Institute of Development Administration

Ammar Siamwalla, Professor
Faculty of Economics
Thammasat University

William Lee Baldwin, Rapporteur
Visiting Professor
Faculty of Economics
Thammasat University

Manfred G. Blobel, Chief
International Bank for Reconstruction and Development
Bangkok

Roger Ernst, Director
U.S. Operations Mission to Thailand

Edgar C. Harrell, Assistant Director for Programs
U.S. Operations Mission to Thailand

Khunthong Intrathai, Professor
Department of Economics and Business Administration
Kasetsart University

W. David Maxwell, Chairman
Dean
College of Liberal Arts
Texas A&M University

William A. McCleary, Visiting Professor
Faculty of Economics
Thammasat University

Narongchai Akrasanee, Dean
Faculty of Economics
Thammasat University

Phisit Pakkasem, Chief
Regional and Urban Planning Division
National Economic and Social Development Board

Priya Osthananda, Director
Foreign Cooperation Division II
Department of Technical and Economic Cooperation

Puey Ungphakorn, Chairman
Prime Minister's Council of Economic Advisors
Rector, Thammasat University

Sakda Saibua, Manager
Research and Planning Department
Bank of Ayudhya Ltd.

Mohandas K. Samuel, Economist
Asian Development Bank
Philippines

Somkiat Ariyapruchya, Economics Officer
Economics Department
Ministry of Foreign Affairs

Snoh Unakul, Secretary General
National Economic and Social
Development Board

Supachai Panitchpakdi, Research
Officer
Bank of Thailand

Sura Sanitanont, Chief Economist
Bangkok Bank Ltd.

Vinyu Vichit-Vadakan, Director
U.N. Asian Institute for Economic
Development and Planning
Bangkok

**Observers**

Robert Bordonaro, Program Coordinator
The Asia Society–SEADAG

Sarah Jane Littlefield, Director
Office of East Asia Affairs
Agency for International Development
Washington

Graham J. Lucas, Representative
Asia Foundation
Bangkok

R.C.G. Martin, First Secretary
Australian Embassy
Bangkok

Charles P. McVicker, Executive
Secretary
The Asia Society–SEADAG

J.A. Peat, Economics Advisor
British Embassy
Bangkok

H.W. Rackl, Second Secretary
Technical & Capital Aid
Embassy of the Federal Republic
of Germany
Bangkok

H.M. Schmid, Deputy Regional
Representative
U.N. Development Program
Bangkok

Shozo Wakabayashi, Secretary
Japanese Embassy
Bangkok

# The Role of Foreign Financial Assistance to Thailand in the 1980s

# 1 Introduction

This account of the Chieng Mai Seminar is organized into seven chapters (including this one). Chapter 2 is devoted to the initial discussion in which an exchange, primarily between Puey and Snoh, sets the stage for much of the subsequent discussion. Chapter 3 is devoted to background papers and the ensuing discussion. These papers were designed to provide for all participants an historical record of the role, extent, and nature of financial aid to Thailand, in order that subsequent papers and discussion might depart from a common base.

In Chapter 4 the participants turn their attention to the future in a very general sense. The dismal scenario of the Amara paper, projecting current economic and demographic trends and conditions so as to arrive at a bleak and dismaying future, provokes heated discussion. The Somkiat paper, predicting a realignment of international relationships and a drastically different international political scene, is scarcely less sobering.

Chapter 5 comprises papers and discussion devoted to more specific aspects of the question of financial aid to Thailand in the 1980s. Financial aid is related to rural development, road construction, education, population control, public health, private foreign investment, and a range of other topics. From the papers and discussion, basic questions emerge. The effect of price movements on economic development far exceeds that of any conceivable level of financial assistance. Can the latter be, then, of any real significance? The achievement of social goals implies a redistribution of resources from the urban to the rural sector. What role can financial aid play in this process? Given developmental goals more complex than the mere maximization of national growth rates, what are the implications for the methods and techniques customarily used to assess the costs and benefits of particular aid-assisted projects? How can financial assistance be most wisely used in the development of the, broadly conceived, human resource? These and other fundamental questions provoke a searching and thorough scrutiny of the role of financial aid in Thailand's economic and social future.

Chapter 6 is devoted to the final "summing up" session of the Seminar, in which the participants attempt to erect a framework that will impart greater coherence and direction to some of their thoughts on the basic topic of the Seminar. The chairman advocates a "three-link" approach concentrating on determination of the developmental needs that financial aid could help to meet, the institutional mechanisms within the country by which financial aid could best be directed to those needs, and the nature and motivations of likely donors.

Mr. Roger Ernst (Director of the U.S. Operations Mission to Thailand) presents a matrix which imparts far greater specificity to each of the three links, and other participants add their concluding remarks and summations.

Chapter 7 attempts to summarize briefly the reactions of the editors of this volume to the papers and discussion. Strengths and weaknesses, as they see them, are presented for consideration.

In seeking papers for the Seminar, the desirability of their having an empirical base was emphasized from the outset. Consequently, the present volume provides not only a collection of analyses of various aspects of the topic, but also a compilation of much of the available data relevant thereto. These data accompany the appropriate paper or summary.

# 2 Setting the Stage: The Initial Discussion

At the outset of the first discussion session, before any papers had been presented, Dr. Puey Ungphakorn struck the basic theme of placing foreign aid in a wider context of Thailand's overall development objectives and problems by suggesting that the Seminar might most usefully begin by considering the views of the Thai government in regard to national development by 1980. What, he asked, did the nation's planning agency, the National Economic and Social Development Board (NESDB), expect Thailand to be like in 1980? In reply, Dr. Snoh Unakul emphasized the need to narrow the existing gaps in income and social structure. These gaps, which external events—such as, the oil crisis and worldwide inflation—were exacerbating, could well destroy the social fabric of the nation. Further, there were social and economic forces in the private sector tending to reinforce the process of widening that the government would have to counteract. For the time being, the government should be giving wholehearted support to the various weaker groups in the society. Later it would have to deal with conflicts within groups, such as labor and agriculture, as their absolute and relative positions improved. For example, a minimum wage might strengthen labor in the modernized sector at the expense of small, traditional business and agriculture. Snoh emphasized that he was speaking for himself and did not know whether the government shared his views and priorities, but he was fairly optimistic.

Puey pushed the question further by asking if the Thai Government intended to follow the development strategy posed for the U.N. Second Development Decade.[a] Did Thailand aim higher or lower than the U.N.? And was the U.N. strategy an appropriate one for Thailand to follow? He noted that the U.N. strategy does not take into account three crucial political parameters: first, whether the Thai Government would evolve into a democracy or revert to

[a]The basic targets of this development strategy are an average growth rate of gross national product of 6 percent per annum (for the less-developed nations), based on an annual transfer of 1 percent of the gross national products of the developed countries. Nations were expected to translate these global targets into individual goals in areas of eradication of illiteracy, raising of nutrition standards, and reduction of the death rate. Report of the Secretary-General of UNCTAD, *The Role of UNCTAD in the Second Development Decade* (New York: United Nations, 1968).

Dr. Puey reviewed the translations made by Thailand. A *per capita* increase in gross national product of 3.5 percent per annum would require lowering the annual rate of population growth to 2.5 percent. Agriculture would have to grow at a rate of 4 percent and industry and services at 8 percent per annum. In the fields of education, health, nutrition, and housing, special attention is to be given to children and women.

military dictatorship; second, whether the insurgency problem would be solved; and third, what Thailand's foreign policy would be by 1980. Snoh was of the opinion that the growth goals posited for the Second Development Decade could be met, assuming reasonable political and social stability. Therefore, there should be more concern given to governmental policies regarding such matters as pricing and profits and issues of social justice which had been relatively neglected in past planning.

This exchange was only the first indication that the participants intended to look at foreign aid from the viewpoint of new aspirations for development. It soon became evident that there was a broadly shared sentiment that future development planning and implementation will be far more complex and difficult than was the case in the past. Economic development will become less important relative to social development. Greater stress must be placed on such matters as more equitable income distribution, social justice, rights of labor, political reform, population control, and rural development involving education, nutrition, health, and industrial relocation as well as per capita productivity. Foreign assistance, either financial or technical, can be of much less help in these efforts than it was in the past in such relatively simple things as the building of roads, dams, and irrigation systems and in controlling certain insect pests. The responsibility and burden will inevitably rest almost entirely on Thailand herself. Yet most of the participants would have agreed with Dr. Supachai Panitchpakdi who asserted in his paper, "Although the development of human resources basically requires the kind of reform which can only be affected by the local authorities, foreign aid can do much to accelerate this process."[b]

The revised papers, as well as the comments on them summarized below, reflect this concern that the newly evolving issues of foreign aid to Thailand can be understood and assessed properly only in connection with recognition of a similarly evolving set of new objectives for development.

---

See p. 127.

# 3 Background

*The first two papers to be presented at the Seminar, by Drs. Phisit and Sakda, were designed to survey and review critically Thailand's past experience with planned development and foreign aid, and also to assess the current situation and present trends. Phisit focused on planning efforts within the Thai Government, explicitly discussing foreign aid only in connection with what he viewed as its rather limited role in financing the nation's development plans. Sakda, on the other hand, reviewed in some detail the history of foreign aid, particularly that from the U.S., noting changes in the objectives and reviewing the actual results. Phisit's paper is presented below, followed by a summary of Sakda's paper and supporting tables and then an account of the subsequent discussion of the two papers.*

# Development Planning and Implementation in Thailand

**Phisit Pakkasem**

## The Evolution of Planning in Thailand

Traditionally, major decisions regarding resource allocation and related economic policy formulation centered in the Ministry of Finance. John Loftus, Economic Advisor to the Ministry of Finance, described resource allocation in the public sector for economic and social development purposes as follows:

> The absence of organized strength behind alternative schemes for economic development, that is to say, the absence of articulate opinion in support of one line of development rather than another [was characteristic]. There was no inherent machinery for resolving conflicts between ministries for funds; with the result that no ministry got enough money to carry out the projects most urgently needed in the sector of economy for which it was responsible.[1]

On the basis of this statement, one can assume that there was no central mechanism for coordinating and planning resource use rationally. Despite efforts to bring about some order, particularly in the allocation of public investments during the preplan period in the 1950s, development efforts in Thailand continued to be unbalanced, uncoordinated, and without long-range direction.

The idea of planned development, which seemed to be the decision-making norm in most developing countries by the end of the 1950s, was not present in the Thai decision-making pattern in this preplan period. Development planning was slow to mature in the minds of the Thai political authorities.[2] There were many reasons for this. First, the Thai economy had been growing steadily with a relatively favorable land-tenure pattern and a good ratio of population-to-resource endowment; therefore, there was no apparent pressure or urgent need for long-range policies in resource allocation. Second, the so-called revolution of rising expectations, which constituted an important sociopolitical force for planned development in many developing nations in Southeast Asia, did not occur with such intensity in Thailand.

However, toward the end of the 1950s a small number of high officials visualized some long-range economic problems in Thailand. In addition, the aid-giving institutions continued to exert increasing pressure on the Thai government to formulate overall development strategies and programs in order to mobilize maximum foreign assistance for implementing public development efforts. The International Bank for Reconstruction and Development (IBRD), in its first overall assessment of the Thai economy, strongly recommended establishment of development planning functions and central machinery at the national level for dealing with long-term development planning in Thailand. Moreover, the IBRD's report pointed out the need for a reorganization of the public administrative structure to make it better suited for development implementation.

The government, under the new leadership of Prime Minister Sarit Dhanarat, announced immediately after this recommendation was made in October, 1958, that one of its top priority goals was to unfold a new economic development program for the nation. The National Economic Development Board (NEDB), charged with central planning functions, was created in July, 1959.

A quantitative comparison of Thailand's three plans is presented in Table 3-1. The First Six-year Plan (1961-1966) and Second Five-year Plan (1967-1971) were formulated and implemented during the decade of the 1960s with the objective of furthering overall economic expansion and developing a better balanced economic structure. Both plans were basically medium-term public expenditure programs to realize overall development objectives. They covered the public development outlays of the central government, foreign grants, and loans. They were concerned mostly with rehabilitation and expansion of the economic and social infrastructure. Major production and financial targets were established; and development strategies, policies, programs, and projects designed to implement these targets were outlined in the plans.

**Table 3-1**
**Overall and Sectoral Growth Targets**

| | First Plan (1961-1966) | | Second Plan (1967-1971) | | Third Plan (1972-1976) | |
|---|---|---|---|---|---|---|
| | Target | Actual | Target | Actual | Target | Actual[a] |
| *Gross Domestic Product (%)* | 5.5 | 8.1 | 8.5 | 7.5 | 7.0 | 5.8 |
| Agriculture | 3.3 | 6.2 | 4.3 | 4.4 | 5.1 | 2.6 |
| Mining & Quarrying | 5.3 | 15.1 | 6.6 | 5.6 | 6.0 | –0.1 |
| Manufacturing | 9.3 | 11.1 | 10.9 | 10.1 | 8.0 | 8.0 |
| Construction | 3.9 | 12.8 | 11.4 | 4.7 | 6.5 | –1.9 |
| Elec & Water Supply | 16.4 | 22.3 | 18.0 | 22.4 | 15.0 | 15.3 |
| Trans, Commun | 9.3 | 6.1 | 11.0 | 7.2 | 6.0 | 6.1 |
| Whlse & Retail Trade | – | 8.1 | 8.4 | 9.1 | 7.0 | 10.1 |
| Banking, Ins & Real Estate | – | 15.8 | 17.0 | 15.4 | 15.0 | 10.8 |
| Ownership of dwellings | 5.4 | 3.1 | 5.0 | 4.2 | 2.5 | 3.3 |
| Pub Admin & Defense | – | 5.4 | 12.0 | 9.5 | 6.0 | 4.4 |
| Services | – | 7.9 | 9.5 | 7.8 | 7.0 | 6.2 |

[a]1972-1973

The First Six-year Plan had several technical weaknesses. For instance, it contained virtually no aggregate analysis. Its overall and sectoral targets were vague. Plan targets were, at best, projections of likely and desirable trends which seemed to correspond with the intentions of the planners. One of the key NEDB planners openly admitted that "the final target was more a forecast than a target. The government was in no position to ensure that the entire program set out would actually be implemented."[3] At the same time, certain substantive components were ignored, especially the regional and manpower implications of the Plan.

The Second Five-year Plan was formulated with considerable technical improvements over the First Plan. It emphasized spatially balanced growth and called attention to regional development programs. The Second Plan also broadened its coverage to include manpower planning and private sector planning, and tested its aggregate projections for internal consistency and reasonableness by the use of macroeconomic models.[4] Its macroeconomic content was improved, compared to the First Plan, and served as a better frame of reference for sectoral planning and development policy formation. The plan size was also affected by resource availability and the absorptive capacity constraint of the public development administration system. The Second Plan was, however, prepared under many uncertainties during the latter part of the 1960s. The problems included a steep rise in the level of U.S. military expenditures in Thailand, sharp changes in the prices of major Thai exports, and rising consumer prices. The economic climate of this period was thus conducive to the adoption of higher growth targets than the First Plan. Another significant innovation of the Second Plan period was the introduction of an annual planning process to draw up an Annual Operations Plan from 1968 onward in order to review and adjust the targets, programs, and projects of the Plan in light of changing conditions.

There was a general consensus that both plans had led to some improvement in resource allocation within the public sector. They brought to bear the various existing ideas on development throughout the public sector, allocating the available public resources with a view to maximum coordinated achievement rather than simply curbing a wide variety of miscellaneous departmental demands. Since most of the public development projects had to be submitted through and evaluated by NEDB, a number of low-priority projects could be removed and public investments could be programed within a longer-term perspective of development objectives. The basic task of rehabilitation and expansion of social overhead capital was accomplished. The foundations for further growth and diversification of the Thai economy, on which the current Third Plan (1972-1976) was to build, had been laid under the first two Plans during the decade of 1960s. These were the real claims to success of the first decade of development planning in Thailand.

The current Third Plan (1972-1976) was prepared and launched when the

Thai economy was undergoing a process of adjustment from rapid growth of the 1960s to a slow pace, with a deteriorating external economic position. These depressive effects were amplified by pessimistic views of private investors due to uncertainty about the future growth of the economy. The Third Plan has thus been designed to solve various economic problems that unavoidably arose in the late 1960s and early 1970s.

The Third Plan emphasizes the need to achieve output and investment growth. One of the main targets is to achieve a real GDP growth rate of 7 percent a year from 1971 to 1976. The Plan regards the balance of payments as the main constraint on future growth and proposes a set of development strategies to relieve this constraint—namely, further expansion and diversification of exports, checking import growth through various fiscal and monetary measures, and larger increases in external capital inflows, both official and private. The Third Plan gives higher priority to agriculture and education than did the First and Second Plans. The emphasis on agriculture reflects a recognition of that sector's potential contribution to export diversification and growth. Another closely linked development objective of the Plan is reduction of spatial or regional income disparities between urban and rural areas, and between the central and other lagging regions. This particular development objective calls for additional development expenditures on agriculture, education, and other social services that would directly benefit rural areas and outlying regions. The Plan also calls for immediate improvement and organization of the public development administration, particularly to increase its effectiveness for plan implementation and for supporting private efforts in the development process.

In summary, two significant developments have already occurred as a result of Thailand's development planning. The first was the creation of a planning structure at the national level. The NEDB has become a new technical component of the public policy decision-making structure, and an agency through which resource allocation power can be increasingly shared. Despite the efforts made in the preparation of the first three plans, which involved a good deal of cooperation between NEDB and many sectoral ministries, overall policy agencies, and international aid donors, there is still room for improvements in the development planning process. These include improvement of individual project preparation, intra and intersectoral planning, the spatial aspect of planning, and planning in several critical areas of economic policy. The second significant development was the explicit adoption of public policy objectives aimed at national development with better resource mobilization and allocation decisions.

## Size of the Plans and Sectoral Priorities

To achieve multiple development objectives and growth targets and to implement public development programs, the current Third Five-year Plan calls for

100 billion baht of public development expenditures, compared to 65 billion baht in the Second Plan and 32 billion baht in the First Plan (Table 3-2). In determining the size of the Third Plan, which is triple that of the First Plan, due consideration has been given both to the expected availability of financial resources and the capital-absorptive capacity of the public sector for effective implementation. The 100 billion baht includes the capital and current expenditures of the central government, local authorities, and state enterprises on programs and projects included in the Plan. Based on the experiences of the first two plans, the overall size of development expenditures seems to be within the Thai government's ability to mobilize sufficient resources from public saving as well as from nonexpansionary domestic and external sources. For the current Third Plan, the size of development outlays would also seem to be feasible if the government sufficiently raises its tax revenue and is capable of greatly increasing its mobilization of external resources. However, the level of public saving is likely to remain low unless the nation's tax effort is increased and the growth of current spending, particularly for security management, is curbed.

From the First to the current Third Plan, the sectoral allocation of public development expenditures indicates shifts in sectoral priorities from emphasis on economic infrastructure to social sectors, whose combined share has increased from 28.5 percent in the First Plan to 42.6 percent in the Second and Third Plans, respectively. Education has recently been given the highest share, with

**Table 3-2**
**Planned Development Expenditures and Sectoral Priorities (Billions of Baht)**

| | First Plan | | Second Plan | | Third Plan | |
|---|---|---|---|---|---|---|
| | Amount | (%) | Amount | (%) | Amount | (%) |
| *Economic Sectors* | | | | | | |
| Agriculture | 4.6 | 14.1 | 10.5 | 15.9 | 13.7 | 13.6 |
| Industry & Mining | 2.6 | 7.9 | 1.1 | 1.7 | 2.4 | 2.4 |
| Trans & Commun | 10.2 | 31.4 | 17.1 | 26.0 | 19.5 | 19.4 |
| Power | 4.3 | 13.3 | 5.0 | 7.6 | 7.9 | 7.9 |
| Subtotal | 21.7 | 66.7 | 33.8 | 51.2 | 43.4 | 43.3 |
| *Social Sectors* | | | | | | |
| Social Dev | 5.5 | 16.7 | 1.9 | 2.9 | 2.7 | 2.7 |
| Urban & Rural | – | – | 8.4 | 12.8 | 14.9 | 14.9 |
| Health | 1.4 | 4.2 | 3.6 | 5.5 | 6.3 | 6.3 |
| Education | 2.5 | 7.6 | 14.1 | 21.4 | 32.9 | 32.8 |
| Subtotal | 9.4 | 28.5 | 28.0 | 42.6 | 56.9 | 56.7 |
| Unallocated | 1.5 | 4.8 | 4.1 | 6.2 | – | – |
| Total | 32.6 | 100.0 | 65.8 | 100.0 | 100.3 | 100.0 |

one-third of the total outlays of the Third Plan, followed by transportation and communication, and agriculture. Shifts in sectoral priorities have been in line with the shift of overall development objectives of the plans. Public policy has become increasingly concerned with the redistributive aspect and the issue of social justice in the process of national development.

## Financing Public Development Expenditures

Choices of growth targets of the three plans have been based not only on analyses of the past trends and potentials of the Thai economy, but also on the resource bases, both domestic and external, which the Thai government could mobilize for financing various public development programs and projects included in the plans. From the point of view of plan implementation, the timely mobilization of financial resources to meet the envisaged target is as important as its required volume.

The performance of the first two plans in resource mobilization has been relatively successful in comparison with most developing countries in the region. The sum total of financial resources mobilized for public development programs and actually spent under the First and Second Plans was approximately 94,064 million baht, short of the projected investment target of 98,259 million baht (Table 3-3). The shortfall in financial implementation could be attributed to several factors, particularly in those programs and projects which involved external financing. These factors included the relative slowness in concluding loan negotiations, the terms of certain bilateral foreign loans which became bottlenecks to the execution of some projects, and the lengthy process of bidding and finalizing contracts. However, a significant part of the shortfall was also due to the capital-absorptive capacity of the public sector. There were

**Table 3-3**
**Planned and Actual Development Expenditures (Millions of Baht)**

| | First Plan (1961-1966) | | Second Plan (1967-1971) | | Third Plan (1972-1976) | |
|---|---|---|---|---|---|---|
| | Target | Actual | Target | Actual | Target | Actual[a] |
| *Financing* | | | | | | |
| Development Expenditure | 32,468 | 27,682 | 65,791 | 66,382 | 100,275 | 34,800 |
| Domestic | 21,830 | 20,029 | 50,438 | 57,135 | 83,345 | 30,149 |
| Foreign | 10,638 | 7,653 | 15,353 | 9,247 | 16,930 | 4,651 |
| Loans | 7,186 | 4,772 | 10,608 | 5,465 | 11,930 | 3,141 |
| Grants | 3,452 | 2,881 | 4,745 | 3,782 | 5,000 | 1,510 |

[a]1972-1973

several changes and modifications of some projects and programs because they had not been properly formulated or phased with complementary projects. Some were also badly mixed with complementary investments in both physical and human capital. In addition, the shortage of certain types of manpower and a lack of development-oriented management competence in several key agencies of the government contributed to the shortfall in financial implementation of the first two plans.

During the course of implementation of the first two plans, there were several administrative reorganizations and some improvements in the field of development administration—particularly in the areas of economic management, development policies, and project preparation—with the aim of improving plan formulation and implementation. The latest administrative reorganization, in October, 1972, was accompanied by a strengthening of the staffs in such key ministries as Agriculture, Industry, and Commerce. The Office of the National Economic Development Board (NEDB) has also been renamed as the National Economic and Social Development Board (NESDB) and is now undergoing a drastic reorganization of its planning structure in order to improve its planning functions and adjust more completely to the changing environment.

Another feature of development financing in Thailand is that the share of domestic financing has been much larger than that of external financing. In terms of total mobilization and uses of resources, both domestic savings and capital formation required for plan implementation in Thailand were among the highest in Southeast Asia. The share of domestic financing in the first two plans was about 82 percent of the total actual development expenditures. The current Third Plan relies slightly less on external financing, such financing being about 17 percent of the total outlays. Approximately 70 percent of public development expenditures during the Third Plan will be financed by central budget appropriations, and 13 percent by the current surpluses of local governments and state enterprises. It is clear that raising the required level of domestic financial resources calls for considerable fiscal efforts and political determination on the part of the government.

So far as external resource mobilization is concerned, the actual amount of foreign loans and grants mobilized and used in the financing of the first two plans fell short of their targets. In particular, foreign loans actually disbursed amounted to only 58 percent of the total projected for both plans, and grants received were 81 percent of the amount envisaged in the plans.

In absolute terms, foreign financing required for the Third Plan is somewhat larger than for the Second Plan; but, as stated earlier, its share of total development outlays declines somewhat. The Third Plan's program of external official borrowing was, however, accepted as a reasonable estimate of the requirements by the Consultative Group for Thailand in 1972. This program originally called for commitments of official loans totaling about 596 million U.S. dollars in 1972-1976. The build-up to this much higher level of commitments requires a considerable effort and continued improvement in project preparation. The government is giving greater emphasis to foreign loan project preparation, including feasibility studies, in order that the delay in loan negotiation can be reduced. In addition to official borrowing from abroad, the Third Plan counts on official grants totaling nearly 250 million U.S. dollars. Priorities are given to education and agriculture.

## The Record of Achievement: Expansion of National Output

One obvious way of measuring the impact of planned development is to examine the degree to which national growth rate targets have been achieved. During the first decade of development planning, Thailand experienced an impressive record of economic growth (Table 3-4 and Figure 3-1). Between 1961 and 1971, Gross Domestic Product (GDP), at constant prices, grew an average of 8 percent annually. The GDP over the First Plan period, 1961-1966, increased at an average annual rate of 8.1 percent as compared to the planned growth target of 5.5 percent. For the Second Plan period the average growth rate was 7.5 percent per annum, which was slightly below the planned target of 8.5 percent. Nevertheless, this was among the highest sustained growth rates of national output in Southeast Asia. GDP doubled during the period from 59 billion baht in 1961 to 127 billion baht in 1971.

The pace of growth accelerated between the first and second halves of the 1960s. In 1966, for instance, the economy showed a rate of growth of 12.2 percent, reflecting a bumper crop of paddy, an increase in public and private investment, and the rapid build-up in U.S. military expenditures in Thailand. Direct and indirect U.S. military expenditures in Thailand since 1965 have had a noticeable impact not only on the overall growth rates, but also on the composition of growth. Construction growth, for instance, reached 20 percent in some years and averaged nearly 13 percent during the period 1965-1969. Some of the service sectors also expanded faster than if demand had come entirely from domestic sources.

During the time of the First and Second Plans, the Thai economy also experienced some structural changes. There was a shift of production away from traditional agriculture toward industrial production, services and raw material exploitation (Figure 3-2). The share of agriculture in GDP decreased from 37.4 percent in 1961 to 29.8 percent in 1971, while industrial production–manufacturing, construction, mining and quarrying, and electricity–increased its share from 20.1 percent to 26.2 percent over the same period. On the expenditure side of the national accounts, there was a gradual shift from consumption to investment. Investment rose from 15 percent of GDP (1960-1962 average) to 24.4 percent in the 1969-1971 period. On the whole, the Thai economy during

**Table 3-4**
**Gross Domestic Product at 1962 Prices (Millions of Baht)**

| | 1961 | 1962 | 1963 | 1964 | 1965 | 1966 | 1967 | 1968 | 1969 | 1970 | 1971 | 1972*p* | 1973*e* |
|---|---|---|---|---|---|---|---|---|---|---|---|---|---|
| Agriculture | 22,062.6 | 23,688.7 | 25,796.9 | 26,123.2 | 27,060.8 | 30,785.3 | 29,904 | 32,799 | 35,257 | 36,174 | 38,112 | 36,929 | 40,136 |
| Crops | 16,317.0 | 17,673.5 | 19,301.9 | 19,146.4 | 19,580.8 | 23,056.2 | 21,033 | 22,856 | 24,542 | 25,139 | 26,658 | 24,812 | 27,343 |
| Livestock | 3,039.9 | 3,099.2 | 3,164.9 | 3,250.9 | 3,341.1 | 3,509.6 | 3,828 | 3,811 | 3,980 | 4,077 | 4,115 | 4,265 | 4,105 |
| Fisheries | 831.1 | 968.7 | 1,242.4 | 1,511.0 | 1,683.2 | 1,951.9 | 2,603 | 3,364 | 4,001 | 4,330 | 4,617 | 5,011 | 5,805 |
| Forestry | 1,873.6 | 1,947.3 | 2,087.7 | 2,214.9 | 2,455.7 | 2,267.6 | 2,440 | 2,768 | 2,734 | 2,628 | 2,722 | 2,841 | 2,883 |
| Mining & Quarrying | 659.0 | 755.7 | 807.8 | 941.0 | 1,193.3 | 1,417.8 | 1,572 | 1,733 | 1,810 | 1,792 | 1,862 | 1,794 | 1,857 |
| Manufacturing | 8,013.3 | 8,997.1 | 9,810.5 | 10,654.5 | 12,354.9 | 13,795.2 | 15,465 | 16,594 | 18,821 | 20,607 | 22,363 | 23,843 | 26,079 |
| Construction | 2,862.6 | 3,270.3 | 3,613.5 | 4,152.1 | 4,612.3 | 5,604.1 | 6,640 | 6,944 | 7,046 | 7,019 | 7,065 | 6,672 | 6,799 |
| Elect & Water Supply | 325.9 | 377.6 | 386.0 | 477.8 | 608.7 | 809.2 | 1,051 | 1,441 | 1,556 | 1,865 | 2,222 | 2,602 | 2,952 |
| Trans & Commun | 4,248.4 | 4,632.9 | 4,795.4 | 5,348.1 | 5,608.5 | 6,013.2 | 6,633 | 6,818 | 7,289 | 8,241 | 8,513 | 8,795 | 9,588 |
| Whlse & Retail Trade | 9,471.7 | 9,897.6 | 10,883.2 | 12,094.8 | 12,823.5 | 14,132.5 | 16,686 | 17,722 | 18,754 | 20,995 | 21,862 | 23,636 | 26,517 |
| Banking, Ins & Real Estate | 1,275.9 | 1,480.3 | 1,613.5 | 1,860.7 | 2,136.3 | 2,620.3 | 3,044 | 3,507 | 4,104 | 4,780 | 5,354 | 5,801 | 6,576 |
| Ownership of Dwellings | 1,655.0 | 1,703.1 | 1,749.6 | 1,802.7 | 1,859.3 | 1,931.3 | 2,006 | 2,092 | 2,201 | 2,294 | 2,374 | 2,448 | 2,531 |
| Pub Admin & Defense | 2,713.6 | 2,847.5 | 3,121.4 | 3,208.3 | 3,457.8 | 3,541.5 | 3,869 | 4,409 | 4,767 | 5,208 | 5,572 | 5,845 | 6,074 |
| Services | 5,742.2 | 6,142.2 | 6,547.5 | 7,029.7 | 7,771.1 | 8,539.2 | 9,266 | 10,227 | 10,941 | 11,753 | 12,427 | 13,256 | 14,018 |
| Gross Domestic Product (GDP) | 59,029.2 | 63,793.0 | 69,125.3 | 73,692.9 | 79,486.5 | 89,189.6 | 96,136 | 104,286 | 112,546 | 120,728 | 127,726 | 131,621 | 143,127 |
| Growth Rate (%) | 5.3 | 8.1 | 8.4 | 6.6 | 7.9 | 12.2 | 7.8 | 8.5 | 7.9 | 7.3 | 5.8 | 3.0 | 8.7 |

*p*: preliminary
*e*: estimated

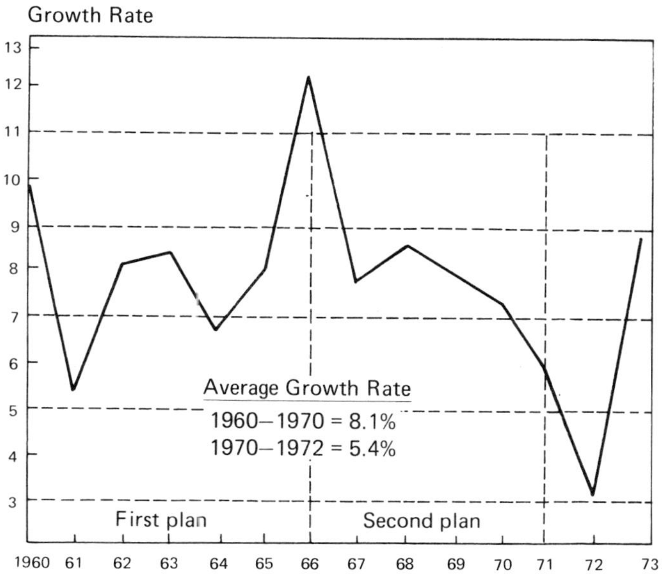


Average Growth Rate

First Plan Period

1961–1963 = 7.2%
1964–1966 = 8.9%
1961–1966 = 8.1%

Second Plan Period

1967–1969 = 8.1%
1970–1971 = 6.5%
1967–1971 = 7.5%

Third Plan Period

1972–1973 = 5.8%

**Figure 3-1**. Economic Growth Rates. Source: NESDB, 1974

the period of the first two plans maintained a remarkably strong resource position. Particularly, rapid growths of domestic savings and export earnings were conspicuous. In terms of financing its own growth, Thailand's savings increased at an annual average of 13.3 percent, and the average growth of exports of goods and services was more than 10 percent per year in the 1960s.

From this aggregate analysis, recent growth in national output under Thailand's first two plans seems to cast a favorable light on the planning process. Undoubtedly, the accelerated growth of aggregate income and production was aided by the rapid increase in public investment directed toward improving the

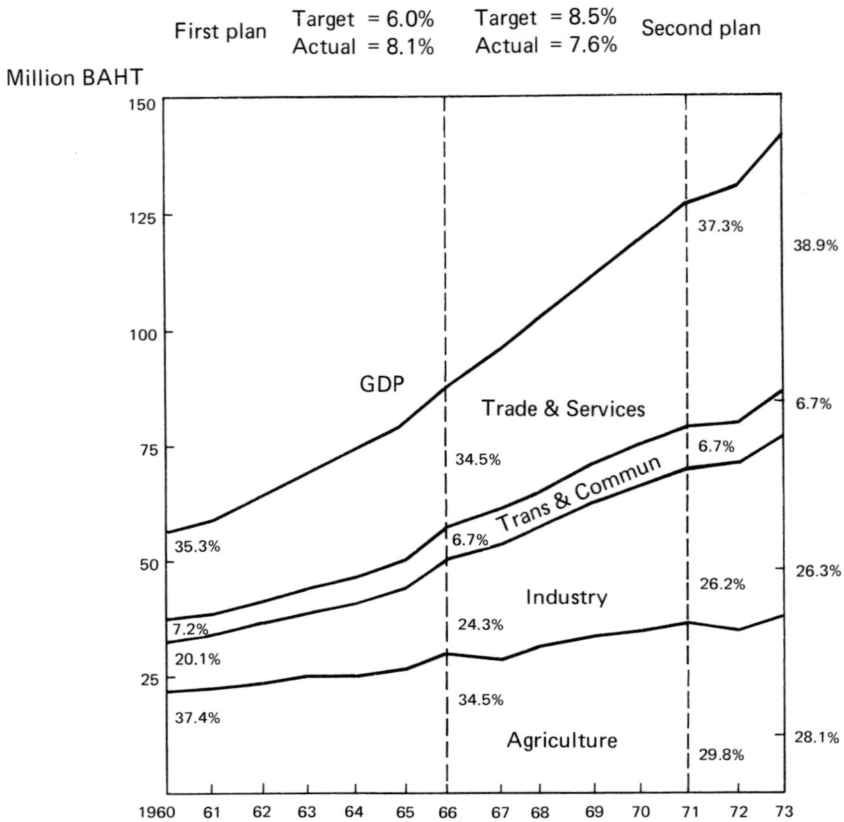


Agriculture
- Crops
- Livestock
- Fisheries
- Forestry

Industry
- Mining & Quarrying
- Manufacturing
- Construction
- Electricity and Water Supply

Services
- Banking
- Wholesale and Retail Trade
- Ownership of Dwellings
- Public Administration and Defense
- Services

**Figure 3-2.** GDP by Sectors at 1962 Prices. Source: NESDB, 1974

country's basic economic and social infrastructures. Both the World Bank and NEDB's evaluation of the two plans gave credit to the government for developing a set of incentives in the use of modern inputs and an appropriate mixture of private and public investments in several sectors. However, it is undeniable that other exogeneous factors–high levels of foreign capital inflows, external demands, and internal political stability—contributed significantly to the national economic growth which involved changes in both the level of and the structure of national output.

However, Thailand began to experience a gradual slowdown of economic growth starting from 1969 and continuing into 1971. Real GDP growth slowed from 7.9 percent in 1969 to 5.8 percent in 1971, and dropped even farther to about 3 percent in 1972. The economic slowdown was triggered by poor export performance and declines in U.S. military spending in Thailand from a peak level equivalent to 4.5 percent of GDP in 1968 to 2.8 percent in 1971. These changes in exogeneous growth determinants affected the economy in many ways, ranging from a sluggish domestic demand to a decline in private investment. By 1970, excess capacity became apparent, particularly in the construction and manufacturing sectors. These depressive effects were amplified by pessimistic views of private investors due to uncertainty about the future growth of the economy. The Third Five-year Plan (1972-1976) was thus prepared and launched during this period of adjustment and uncertainty.

From mid-1972, however, an economic recovery has been underway, triggered by steeply rising exports due to abrupt shifts from surplus to shortage on the world's markets for three Thai products, namely, rice, sugar and kenaf. In 1972, gross capital inflows began to rise again with the recovery of private investment. Investment expenditures began to rise and gain further momentum in 1973. Domestic demand began to pick up, and the growth of national output was approximately 8.7 percent in 1973. With recent improvement in total output of the Thai economy, the outlook for the remaining period of the Third Plan seems to indicate that the Plan's target for GDP growth of 7 percent is within reach.

## The Record of Achievement: Balance of Payments

A summary of balance of payments positions during the first two plans (1961-1971), given in Table 3-5, shows clearly that Thailand had no significant deficit throughout the period. The net capital inflow into Thailand has continuously been in excess of the amounts required to finance the current deficit. The summation of the current deficits between 1961-1971 was 1,486 million U.S. dollars whereas Thailand obtained net capital inflows of 1,855 million U.S. dollars. As a consequence, foreign exchange reserves were strengthened to the extent that net capital inflows exceeded the deficit by over 369 million U.S. dollars. In 1971, the total foreign exchange reserves of Thailand stood at 722 million U.S. dollars.

During the Second Plan period, the balance of payments deficit totaled 127 million U.S. dollars. The turning point in the balance of payments came in 1969

**Table 3-5**
**First and Second Plan—Balance of Payments (Million U.S. Dollars)**

| | First Plan 1961-1966 | Second Plan 1967-1971 | Total 1961-1971 |
|---|---|---|---|
| 1. *Goods & Services* | | | |
| Receipts | 4,040 | 5,609 | 9,649 |
| Payments | 4,354 | 6,781 | 11,135 |
| Net Goods & Services | −314 | −1,172 | −1,486 |
| 2. *Transfers, Net* | 247 | 284 | 531 |
| 3. *Capital, Net* | 404 | 559 | 963 |
| 4. Error & Omissions, Net | 159 | 202 | 361 |
| 5. *Change in Reserves* | 496 | −127 | 369 |
| 6. Reserves Level at the end of Each Plan Period | 849 | 722 | |

when foreign exchange reserves fell for the first time, by about 48 million U.S. dollars. Reserves continued to fall over the next two years, by 132 million U.S. dollars in 1970, and by 17 million U.S. dollars in 1971.

This decline was due to the combination of rapid growth of imports and sluggish merchandise exports. The weak performance of exports was due largely to a drop in rice exports, coupled with substantial price reductions in the period 1969-1971. Although some progress was made in export diversification, especially in crops, this could not compensate for the deterioration in rice exports. At the same time, in 1969, net capital inflows (especially public capital inflows) began to decline and could not compensate for the current account deficit. Reserves began to decline for the first time in 1969 and continued to do so through 1971.

The balance of payments improved markedly again from mid-1972 when the Third Plan was underway. This was triggered by steeply rising exports which showed an unexpectedly large increase of 32 percent in 1972. The increase in exports was due mainly to special factors, namely, the abrupt shifts from surplus to shortage on the international markets for three Thai products, rice, sugar and kenaf. Shifts in world demand for these three commodities were accompanied by increases in both quantities and prices from 1972 onward.

## Prospects for the Period 1974-1976

The recent economic recovery in Thailand and the outlook for the remainder of the Third Plan period, 1974-1976, seem to indicate that the overall growth target of 7 percent a year will be within reach. Although the growth potential of the Thai economy may exceed 7 percent, this growth target has been chosen in order to attain a reasonable growth path, and at the same time bring about a better interregional balance in welfare, in accordance with the Plan's emphasis on the distributive aspect of development. However, Thailand's economic growth beyond 1974 will also be influenced by factors outside the control of government, namely, world price behavior and the energy crisis, which have already contributed to the increased inflationary trend in Thailand. This may not only slow down the rate of economic growth, but may also lower Thailand's competitive position in the international market and adversely affect the standard of living.

In general, the balance of payments will continue to be a major constraint in future GDP growth for Thailand. If recent improvement in the balance of payments continues, foreign exchange reserves will probably stay above the Plan forecast. The government will have to continue stepping up its efforts to promote investment and production for export, as well as proceed with various key policy reforms, especially in fiscal, monetary, and pricing policies. There is no doubt that a further acceleration of exports will depend on the already-mentioned external factors as well as on the Thai government's ability to institutionalize the policy changes. In addition, future political development and stability will play an important role in determining Thailand's future prospects for achieving its various development objectives and continuing its societal changes.

## Notes

1. Thailand Economic Survey Group, "Report on Economic Development Plans," (Bangkok: Ministry of Finance, Mimeographed 1957), p. 11.

2. Prayad Buranasiri and Snoh Unakul, "Obstacles to Effective Planning Encountered in the Thai Planning Experience," *The Philippine Economic Journal*, Vol. IV (August, 1965), p. 336.

3. Snoh Unakul, *Fiscal and Monetary Policies and Thai Planning Process* (Bangkok: National Economic Development Board, 1971), Chapter 27.

4. National Economic Development Board, "The Methodology for Preparing the Second Economic and Social Development Plan of Thailand," (Bangkok: NEDB, Mimeographed May, 1967), p. 2.

# The History of Foreign Aid to Thailand: A Summary of Sakda Saibua's Paper

Sakda's paper reviewed foreign aid to Thailand since World War II both by source and sectoral activity. He noted that, while the U.S. had been the single largest combined donor and lender, the International Bank for Reconstruction and Development (IBRD), the U.N., and the Colombo Plan nations had been important multilateral donors and that significant bilateral assistance or loans had been received from the Federal Republic of Germany, France, the Netherlands, Denmark, and Japan. In discussing foreign aid, Sakda explicitly excluded military aid from the U.S. which he did observe amounted to 0.8 billion U.S. dollars and represented roughly 60 percent of the Thai government's budget for defense. The bulk of grant aid has been for technical assistance. Loans have been concentrated in power, irrigation, and roads. Sakda then reviewed aid to agriculture, infrastructure, industry, public administration, education and public health, and rural development and security, each in some detail. He concluded that aid to agriculture had been quite successful, primarily because it was aimed from the beginning at clearly defined targets such as seed improvement, pest eradication, irrigation, and diversification. Similarly, both technical advice and loans were of significance in infrastructure development. In public health, foreign aid was effective in assisting in the eradication and control of communicable diseases, but aid efforts led to very little progress in supplying health services to rural areas. In education, little was achieved; while in public administration, the programs were on the whole successful because they were well conceived and directed at fairly specific and technical programs of modernization of fiscal management, economic planning and statistics, and advanced training in public administration. Sakda concluded that foreign aid had been most useful in programs in which transfer of relatively simple technology was the key to success and in which specific needs had been identified. On the other hand, the less successful projects were those which required significant institutional changes to achieve their objectives.

Sakda's analysis and evaluation were supported by the statistical tables presented at the conclusion of the discussion.

## Discussion: The Phisit and Sakda Papers

While Phisit's paper concerned itself with past and present planning in Thailand—in accord with his assignment—both his own observations and the related comments of others at the Seminar focused more on the future.

In presenting his paper, Phisit called attention to the shift in Thai planning from concern with growth, production, and infrastructure to concern with problems of income distribution and social justice. Emphasis is now being placed on local and regional structure rather than on national structure. National planning has become a social and political process as well as an economic one. Hence, success depends on political support and on the abilities of the planners to adjust to political changes. Turning to what Thailand might look like by the year 2000, Phisit expressed the hope that planning could concern itself with such complex issues as the environment, urban problems, land use, water-resource development, and population, all of which would require a very long-range perspective in working out the fourth, fifth and sixth plans of four or five years' duration each over the next two decades. Donor nations have avoided giving aid directly to political development, he concluded, but aid to certain types of social and economic projects can be a key factor in strengthening political development.

Before opening the floor to a general discussion of Phisit's paper, the Chairman asked Snoh and Preeya to comment on Sakda's paper, since both papers dealt with aspects of the background to a consideration of present and future foreign aid and since Sakda was unable to be present for the discussion of his paper.

Snoh, in reviewing Sakda's paper for the Seminar, emphasized the question of the need for foreign assistance. If such need is strong, as Snoh in fact believes to be the case, then the declining amount of aid is a basic problem. But following up on Sakda's conclusion that aid which required institutional change had not been effective, Snoh noted that Thailand's absorptive capacity in the currently stressed social sectors may be limited. There must be institutional reform within the bureaucracy to increase this capacity. Further, projects undertaken must be of benefit to the Thai people, which unfortunately was not always the case in the past. In Snoh's opinion, both Thai and donor agencies must share the blame for past deficiencies in this regard.

An additional problem seen by Snoh is that Thai engineers and other professionals are not given a fair chance to obtain employment on aid-financed projects. NESDB was at the time preparing recommendations to the Cabinet on measures to encourage Thai consultants to participate in foreign aid project activities.

Snoh also remarked that there has been a reaction among influential elements in the country against the acceptance of any foreign aid, and it will be important for academicians, the press, and intellectual leaders to mobilize public understanding and support for continued aid.

Preeya noted that Sakda's paper gave the impression that foreign aid had been important in the economic development of Thailand. She did not dispute this, but she observed that it has also contributed to confusion in development planning. Aid from the U.S. has been declining since 1968 but will probably remain the major source of foreign assistance to Thailand through 1980. Private foundations may become more important. Any effort to coordinate aid and lessen the confusion it engenders must involve the foundations if it is to have any hope of success. Thailand, Preeya continued, has graduated from conceptually simple foreign aid needs to more complex ones. She concluded with a question: Should Thailand, therefore, "play it safe" by continuing to accept aid in the old, tested ways, or should the nation launch new and more risky ventures with new types of foreign aid projects and programs?

Ensuing discussion of both Phisit's and Sakda's papers covered several issues and questions. Snoh's statement that there was a continuing need for aid and his plea that influential nongovernmental figures be enlisted to speak out on its behalf were challenged. It was not clear to at least two members of the Seminar that those who opposed a continuation of foreign aid were entirely wrong. They argued that, if Thai agencies were not capable of identifying suitable programs and projects themselves, but rather had to rely on donors to choose the means and objectives of aid, then perhaps the nation would in fact be better off without such aid—or in any event, the arguments of those opposing aid cannot be lightly dismissed. The immediate need for action planning in a long-run context of the population, food, and employment prospects for the year 2000, as pointed out by Phisit, was strongly endorsed. The treatment of long-term, low-interest loans as *de facto* substitutes for grants was recommended by one of the participants from an aid-giving agency. In his opinion, there was in reality only a bookkeeping difference between a long-term 2 or 3 percent loan and a grant: At least, there was no sound reason why there should be any differences in the types of programs or projects properly funded from these two sources. It was noted that international interdependence will be increasing from now until the year 2000, putting new demands on the abilities of developing nations to absorb flows of technology and new forms of capital; and it was suggested that this is an aspect of Snoh's concern with absorptive capacity that may transcend current concepts of aid.

The tables that were used to support the analysis and conclusions of the Sakda paper are presented here.

**Table 3-6**
**GDP, Total Government Expenditures from Internal Resources and Total Foreign Aid, 1951-1970 (Current Prices, Million U.S. Dollars)**

| | | | | Total Foreign Aid as % of | |
|---|---|---|---|---|---|
| Year | GDP | Total Gov't Expd | Total Foreign Aid | GDP | Total Gov't Expd |
| 1951 | 1,328.6 | 157.4 | 4.1 | 0.3 | 2.6 |
| 1952 | 1,513.9 | 190.5 | 11.0 | 0.7 | 5.8 |
| 1953 | 1,674.9 | 221.9 | 11.6 | 0.7 | 5.2 |
| 1954 | 1,708.9 | 232.8 | 8.4 | 0.5 | 3.6 |
| 1955 | 1,916.9 | 248.5 | 30.1 | 1.6 | 12.1 |
| 1956 | 2,041.6 | 278.6 | 42.0 | 2.1 | 15.1 |
| 1957 | 2,099.2 | 275.1 | 60.0 | 2.9 | 21.8 |
| 1958 | 2,183.8 | 277.7 | 38.4 | 1.8 | 13.8 |
| 1959 | 2,281.7 | 304.6 | 63.0 | 2.8 | 20.7 |
| 1960 | 2,595.4 | 357.9 | 63.4 | 2.5 | 17.7 |
| 1961 | 2,835.1 | 388.8 | 64.1 | 2.3 | 16.5 |
| 1962 | 3,067.0 | 459.7 | 102.9 | 3.4 | 22.4 |
| 1963 | 3,273.0 | 527.5 | 96.7 | 3.0 | 18.3 |
| 1964 | 3,589.8 | 580.3 | 80.6 | 2.2 | 13.9 |
| 1965 | 4,053.0 | 662.3 | 69.0 | 1.7 | 10.4 |
| 1966 | 4,873.8 | 770.5 | 67.6 | 1.4 | 8.8 |
| 1967 | 5,203.1 | 907.9 | 90.7 | 1.7 | 10.0 |
| 1968 | 5,639.8 | 1,079.7 | 146.1 | 2.6 | 13.5 |
| 1969 | 6,279.5 | 1,171.1 | 104.2 | 1.7 | 8.9 |
| 1970 | 6,503.8 | 1,208.3 | 95.1 | 1.5 | 7.9 |
| Total | 64,662.8 | 10,301.1 | 1,249.0 | 1.9 | 12.1 |

Source: NEDB, working papers.

**Table 3-7**
**U.S. Military Aid to Thailand, 1951-1969 (Commitments, Million U.S. Dollars)**

| Year | Regular U.S. Military Assistance | Thai Govt Defense Budget Expenditures | U.S. Military Aid as % of Thai Defense Budget |
|---|---|---|---|
| 1951 | 4.5 | 12.3 | 37 |
| 1952 | 12.0 | 18.2 | 66 |
| 1953 | 56.0 | 21.8 | 257 |
| 1954 | 39.0 | 28.7 | 136 |
| 1955 | 40.0 | 26.1 | 153 |
| 1956 | 43.0 | 37.9 | 113 |
| 1957 | 26.0 | 35.8 | 73 |
| 1958 | 20.0 | 32.9 | 61 |
| 1959 | 18.0 | 69.4 | 26 |
| 1960 | 24.0 | 66.7 | 36 |
| 1961 | 49.0 | 69.2 | 70 |
| 1962 | 88.0 | 76.4 | 115 |
| 1963 | 71.8 | 80.7 | 89 |
| 1964 | 35.2 | 85.7 | 41 |
| 1965 | 30.8 | 69.1 | 32 |
| 1966 | 42.3 | 108.5 | 39 |
| 1967 | 59.0 | 131.5 | 45 |
| 1968 | 76.5 | 176.7 | 43 |
| 1969 | 73.5 | 192.1 | 38 |
| Total | 808.6 | 1,339.7 | 60.4 |

Source: Senate, Security Commitments Abroad, Thailand, pp. 633-34.

**Table 3-8**
**Gross Foreign Borrowings by Thailand, 1951-1970 (Disbursements, Million U.S. Dollars)**

| Year | Government Borrowings: Direct Obligations | Government Borrowings: Repayment Guaranteed | Exchange Availability Insured | Private Suppliers' Credits | Total |
|---|---|---|---|---|---|
| 1951 | 3.7 | 1.0 | – | – | 4.7 |
| 1952 | 8.9 | – | 0.8 | – | 9.7 |
| 1953 | 8.2 | – | 0.7 | – | 8.9 |
| 1954 | 1.8 | 6.1 | 20.7 | – | 28.6 |
| 1955 | 2.0 | 6.9 | 6.3 | – | 15.2 |
| 1956 | 6.8 | 33.3 | 0.6 | – | 40.7 |
| 1957 | 6.3 | 13.5 | 3.6 | – | 23.4 |
| 1958 | 0.3 | 5.2 | 1.0 | – | 6.5 |
| 1959 | 1.6 | 18.8 | – | 4.7 | 25.1 |
| 1960 | 4.0 | 24.0 | – | 3.8 | 31.8 |
| 1961 | 7.3 | 24.9 | 2.9 | 7.1 | 42.2 |
| 1962 | 1.6 | 43.2 | 12.8 | 16.2 | 73.8 |
| 1963 | 2.5 | 39.1 | 1.5 | 17.5 | 60.6 |
| 1964 | 15.8 | 22.2 | 0.2 | 44.3 | 82.5 |
| 1965 | 16.0 | 19.3 | – | 40.2 | 75.5 |
| 1966 | 19.8 | 18.6 | – | 53.0 | 91.4 |
| 1967 | 26.2 | 11.0 | – | 93.0 | 130.2 |
| 1968 | 34.6 | 10.7 | – | 98.5 | 143.8 |
| 1969 | 21.4 | 12.6 | – | 141.9 | 175.9 |
| 1970 | 28.8 | 6.6 | – | 158.6 | 194.0 |
| Total | 217.6 | 317.0 | 51.1 | 678.8 | 1264.5 |

Source: Bank of Thailand, Research Department.

**Table 3-9**

**Distribution by Source and Purpose of Foreign Loans to Thailand, 1950-1970 (Commitments, Million U.S. Dollars)**

| Purpose of Loan | World Bank | U.S. | Ger. | Jap. | Canada | U.K. | Italy | Belgium | Austria | Asian Dev. Bank | Total | (%) |
|---|---|---|---|---|---|---|---|---|---|---|---|---|
| 1. Railways | 14.6 | 1.9 | 20.2 | 7.8 | – | – | – | – | – | – | 44.5 | 7.2 |
| 2. Irrigation | 75.0 | 15.6 | – | 13.4 | – | – | 0.7 | – | 0.8 | – | 105.5 | 17.1 |
| 3. Port | 15.7 | 1.7 | – | 2.7 | – | – | – | – | – | – | 20.1 | 3.3 |
| 4. Power | 130.1 | 44.0 | 40.4 | 23.5 | – | 2.2 | 3.7 | – | 3.4 | – | 247.3 | 40.2 |
| 5. Roads | 103.0 | 0.3 | – | – | – | – | – | – | – | – | 103.3 | 16.8 |
| 6. Industry | 2.5 | 0.7 | 15.2 | – | – | – | – | – | – | 15.0 | 33.4 | 5.4 |
| 7. Telecommunications | – | 13.6 | 6.3 | 12.5 | – | – | – | 2.4 | – | – | 34.8 | 5.7 |
| 8. Education | 6.0 | – | – | – | 1.0 | – | – | – | – | – | 7.0 | 1.1 |
| 9. Others | – | 19.8 | – | – | – | – | – | – | – | – | 19.8 | 3.2 |
| Total | 346.9 | 97.6 | 82.1 | 59.9 | 1.0 | 2.2 | 4.4 | 2.4 | 4.2 | 15.0 | 615.7 | 100.0 |
| (%) | 56.3 | 15.9 | 13.3 | 9.7 | 0.2 | 0.4 | 0.7 | 0.4 | 0.7 | 2.4 | 100.0 | |

Source: DTEC, Office of the Prime Minister.

**Table 3-10**
**Technical Assistance to Thailand by Source, 1951-1970 (Thousand U.S. Dollars)**

| Year | U.S. | U.N. | Colombo Plan | Other Countries | Volunteers | Total |
|---|---|---|---|---|---|---|
| 1951-1960 | 115,488 | n/a | 4,142[a] | 718[b] | n/a | 120,348 |
| 1961 | 6,890 | 1,871 | 2,265 | 460 | 2 | 11,488 |
| 1962 | 12,577 | 3,102 | 3,503 | 607 | 408 | 20,197 |
| 1963 | 17,333 | 1,925 | 3,734 | 684 | 786 | 24,462 |
| 1964 | 12,686 | 3,163 | 3,251 | 713 | 512 | 20,325 |
| 1965 | 18,600 | 3,114 | 2,968 | 1,425 | 868 | 26,975 |
| 1966 | 44,457 | 3,190 | 4,423 | 2,234 | 1,007 | 55,311 |
| 1967 | 56,639 | 4,384 | 5,542 | 3,885 | 1,329 | 71,779 |
| 1968 | 50,328 | 4,215 | 4,474 | 3,350 | 1,438 | 63,805 |
| 1969 | 37,872 | 4,565 | 3,932 | 3,279 | 1,876 | 51,524 |
| 1970 | 30,725 | 5,369 | 6,721 | 4,660 | 2,284 | 49,759 |
| Total | 403,595 | 34,898 | 44,955 | 22,015 | 10,510 | 515,973 |
| (%) | 78.2 | 6.8 | 8.7 | 4.3 | 2.0 | 100 |

[a]CY. 1954-1960

[b]CY. 1959-1960

Source: Department of Technical and Economic Cooperation, Office of the Prime Minister.

**Table 3-11**
**Total Technical Assistance to Thailand by Source and Type, 1967-1972 (Thousand U.S. Dollars)**

| Source / Type | Experts | Fellowships | Equipment | Others | Total | Distribution |
|---|---|---|---|---|---|---|
| AID | 77,815.8 | 16,919.4 | 119,652.4 | – | 214,387.6 | 67.3 |
| U.N. | 16,063.7 | 3,969.5 | 8,371.2 | 2,202.7 | 30,607.1 | 9.6 |
| Colombo Plan | 11,834.1 | 8,098.9 | 14,320.0 | – | 34,253.0 | 10.8 |
| Third Countries | 11,927.6 | 8,947.5 | 5,095.6 | – | 25,970.7 | 8.2 |
| Volunteers | 13,144.6 | – | – | – | 13,144.6 | 4.1 |
| Total | 130,785.8 | 37,935.3 | 147,430.2 | 2,202.7 | 318,363.0 | 100.0 |
| (%) | 41.1 | 11.9 | 46.3 | 0.7 | 100 | |

Source: DTEC, Office of the Prime Minister.

**Table 3-12**
**Technical Assistance by Sector and Source, 1967-1972 (Thousand U.S. Dollars)**

| | U.S. | | U.N. | | Colombo Plan | | Third Countries | | Volunteers | | Total | |
|---|---|---|---|---|---|---|---|---|---|---|---|---|
| Sector | Amount | (%) | Amount | (%) | Amount | (%) | Amount | (%) | Amount | (%) | Amount | (%) |
| Agriculture | 17,911.7 | 8.4 | 7,425.5 | 24.3 | 5,415.2 | 15.8 | 5,561.6 | 21.4 | 152.5 | 1.2 | 36,466.5 | 11.5 |
| Industry | 3,107.7 | 1.4 | 4,591.4 | 15.0 | 422.1 | 1.2 | 1,235.5 | 4.8 | 1.3 | – | 9,358.0 | 2.9 |
| Power | – | – | 733.9 | 2.4 | 555.2 | 1.6 | 1,235.8 | 4.8 | 20.6 | 0.1 | 2,545.5 | 0.8 |
| Commun | 2,376.6 | 1.1 | 2,022.4 | 6.6 | 13,325.2 | 38.9 | 398.1 | 1.5 | – | – | 18,122.3 | 5.7 |
| Health | 22,429.8 | 10.5 | 6,916.0 | 22.6 | 2,300.3 | 6.7 | 1,175.9 | 4.5 | 2,768.3 | 21.0 | 35,590.3 | 11.2 |
| Education | 13,529.3 | 6.3 | 5,494.8 | 18.0 | 6,886.8 | 20.1 | 12,291.6 | 47.3 | 8,763.0 | 66.7 | 46,965.5 | 14.7 |
| Community & Social Dev | 58,789.7 | 27.4 | 2,025.1 | 6.6 | 2,257.3 | 6.6 | 1,429.1 | 5.5 | 1,011.0 | 7.7 | 65,512.2 | 20.6 |
| Administration | 4,636.4 | 2.2 | 897.9 | 2.9 | 1,219.6 | 3.6 | 1,886.2 | 7.3 | 36.6 | 0.3 | 8,676.7 | 2.7 |
| Public Safety | 59,226.2 | 27.6 | – | – | – | – | – | – | – | – | 59,226.2 | 18.6 |
| Unclassified | 32,380.1 | 15.1 | 500.0 | 1.6 | 1,871.4 | 5.5 | 757.0 | 2.9 | 391.3 | 3.0 | 35,899.8 | 11.3 |
| Total | 214,387.5 | 100.0 | 30,607.0 | 100.0 | 34,253.1 | 100.0 | 25,970.8 | 100.0 | 13,144.6 | 100.0 | 318,363.0 | 100.0 |

Source: DTEC, Office of the Prime Minister.

**Table 3-13**
**Participant Training Under U.S. Supported Programs for the Period 1951-1971**

| | Place of Training | | | |
|---|---|---|---|---|
| Fields | U.S. | U.S. & Third Countries | Third Countries | Total |
| Mekong and Pamong | 16 | – | – | 16 |
| Jusmag | 47 | – | – | 47 |
| General | 228 | 4 | 25 | 257 |
| Social Dev | 139 | 21 | 691 | 851 |
| Public Administration | 616 | 53 | 280 | 949 |
| Civil Police | 631 | 1 | 371 | 1,003 |
| Education | 1,212 | 50 | 453 | 1,715 |
| Health | 613 | 67 | 647 | 1,327 |
| Labor | 46 | – | – | 46 |
| Trans | 314 | 6 | 18 | 338 |
| Industry | 247 | 5 | 37 | 289 |
| Agriculture | 790 | 26 | 1,121 | 1,937 |
| Total | 4,899 | 233 | 3,643 | 8,775 |

Source: USOM, Training Division.

**Table 3-14**
**U.N. Assistance by Program, 1967-1972 (Thousand U.S. Dollars)**

| Program | Value (Total) | (%) |
|---|---|---|
| UNDP | 20,313.3 | 66.4 |
| Regular Program | 4,008.8 | 13.1 |
| UNICEF | 5,741.4 | 18.7 |
| Regional & Interregional | 543.5 | 1.8 |
| Total | 30,607.0 | 100.0 |

Source: DTEC, Office of the Prime Minister.

**Table 3-15**
**Colombo Plan Assistance by Country, 1967-1972**

| Country | Value (Total) | (%) |
|---|---|---|
| Australia | 13,277.0 | 38.8 |
| Canada | 2,020.4 | 5.9 |
| U.K. | 4,481.5 | 13.1 |
| New Zealand | 4,065.0 | 11.9 |
| Jap. | 10,066.4 | 29.4 |
| India | 292.7 | 0.8 |
| Singapore | 2.2 | – |
| Malaysia | 31.6 | 0.1 |
| Philippines | 11.2 | – |
| Korea | 5.1 | – |
| Total | 34,253.1 | 100.0 |

Source: DTEC, Office of the Prime Minister.

**Table 3-16**
**Third Countries Assistance by Country, 1967-1972 (Thousand U.S. Dollars)**

| Country | Value (Total) | (%) |
|---|---|---|
| Ger. | 9,487.0 | 36.5 |
| France | 2,859.8 | 11.0 |
| Netherlands | 1,278.7 | 4.9 |
| Denmark | 1,641.9 | 6.3 |
| Austria | 470.1 | 1.8 |
| Israel | 447.0 | 1.7 |
| Belgium | 23.0 | 0.1 |
| Italy | 67.6 | 0.3 |
| Switzerland | 61.1 | 0.2 |
| Greece | 19.2 | 0.1 |
| Norway | 231.5 | 1.0 |
| Sweden | 89.4 | 0.3 |
| The Rep of China | 1,126.3 | 4.3 |
| The UAR | 3.2 | – |
| Foundations & Universities | 8,159.4 | 31.5 |
| The Rep of Korea | 2.8 | – |
| Iran | 2.6 | – |
| Total | 25,970.6 | 100.0 |

Source: DTEC, Office of the Prime Minister.

**Table 3-17**
**Volunteer Assistance by Source, 1967-1972 (Thousand U.S. Dollars)**

| Source | No. | M/M | Value | (%) (Value) |
|---|---|---|---|---|
| PCV | 1,881 | 17,896 | 9,161.8 | 69.7 |
| GVS | 235 | 2,527 | 1,369.2 | 10.4 |
| CUSO | 254 | 2,222 | 1,495.6 | 11.4 |
| VSO | 201 | 1,450 | 735.1 | 5.6 |
| VSA | 84 | 959 | 382.9 | 2.9 |
| Total | 2,655 | 25,054 | 13,144.6 | 100.0 |

PVC: Peace Corps Volunteer (U.S.).
GVS: German Volunteer Service.
CUSO: Canadian University Service Overseas.
VSO: Volunteer Service Overseas (U.K.).
VSA: Volunteer Service Agency (New Zealand).

Source: DTEC, Office of the Prime Minister.

# 4 Future Perspectives

*As the title of Dr. Amara's paper indicates, his study deals primarily with the role of public administration in coping with Thailand's problems through the 1980s and the contribution that foreign aid can make in developing a public administrative capability adequate to deal with these problems. However, the "scenario" presented in the third section of his paper attracted a great deal of attention at the Seminar in its own right, and was the focal point of a great deal of discussion both related to the rest of the paper and otherwise. This grim scenario provided a logical backdrop for a series of crucial questions. Was Amara's projection a reasonable forecast? If so, could the dismal future he described be prevented from actually occurring by actions taken now? By what sorts of actions? And what, if any, contributions could be made in this respect by foreign aid? Amara himself was prepared to defend his forecast as an accurate projection of existing trends and conditions, drawn from his work and that of a group of colleagues serving as an interdisciplinary committee. "I don't paint, I calculate," he stated. He would, of course, be happy to be proved wrong, but he regards his projections for the 1980s as an accurate depiction of the set of conditions and problems public administrators in Thailand may expect to face at that time.*

*Dr. Somkiat, whose paper could not be prepared for publication in time for inclusion in this volume, also made a forecast of the future as a part of his study; but his predictions dealt with international relations and the international power structure likely to be facing Southeast Asia in the 1980s, which Thailand would at that time have to be taking into account in fashioning her foreign policies and aid strategies. Thus the Seminar was presented with quite plausible and significant scenarios of both the domestic and international situations within which foreign aid to Thailand might be given and received ten years in the future.*

# Foreign Aid to Public Administration in Thailand in the 1980s

**Amara Raksasataya**

## Introduction

Foreign aid has undergone spectacular changes. At the end of World War II, the victorious countries, especially the U.S., were emotionally moved to assist the countries of Europe to extricate themselves from the catastrophe of war. Ensuing development of the cold war between the free world and socialist countries led to the formation of alliance systems. To induce the economically weaker nations to become their partners, the leading countries of both camps were willing to spend liberally on military, economic, and technical development programs financed primarily by free grants and bilateral loans. The recipient countries, in their rush toward economic progress, were more than willing to receive this aid, with very few reservations.

By the late 1960s and more visibly in the early 1970s, foreign aid, especially of a bilateral nature, became a touchy issue. Citizens and politicians of the developed countries began to voice dissatisfaction with the mounting cost of the ever-expanding, seemingly unending aid to a long list of unworthy governments. The developing countries also were not entirely happy. While the authorities in these countries were in general eager for more assistance, the intellectuals were becoming increasingly restive. In some countries, foreign aid was viewed as a means of perpetuating military dictatorships, and in many it was considered demeaning to live on handouts from the richer countries. To the advocates of self-reliance and self-respect, "foreign aid" thus became an unpopular term. Bilateral aid was considered the worst because of the prevalence of specific conditions or "strings" in this form of aid. Multilateral loans at concessional rates, while much sought after, were criticized for the very fact that they are concessional or "soft"–as unfair to the individuals and private financial institutions that have to compete for funding in regular markets. Private investment from foreign countries or multinational corporations seems to be the wave of the future, but it, too, will be seen to have great shortcomings.

Against such a virulent background, the preparation of this paper is indeed a difficult mental exercise. The title of the paper implies that there will be assistance from foreign countries to Thailand in the 1980s which will be devoted to public administration. It presupposes that Thailand, then as well as now, will need such assistance. Though the Thais have been giving aid to other countries–especially in the Asian region–in various areas of public administration, the paper will not deal with this interchange. To help overcome the bad image that foreign aid possesses, this paper should perhaps be retitled "External Inputs to the Development of Public Administration in Thailand." Whatever the preferred title, the paper will project and describe in a straightforward fashion an average annual need (not implying that assistance to meet this need is desirable, nor suggesting minimum-maximum levels at which this need might be met), for foreign aid in the 1980s based on past trends and possible future developments in Thailand (which, in turn, depend on several "ifs" or actions which Thailand may be taking between now and the projected period of the 1980s).

In view of the mounting criticism of foreign aid from several quarters, it might be desirable to think, write, or convene seminars of experts to discuss such topics as "Planning for Total Self-reliance in the 1980s–Mobilization of Thai Resources," "Toward Healthier International Interchange of Resources, or Liberating Resource–rich, Underdeveloped Countries from Exploitation by Developed Countries." Be that as it may, this paper will attempt to apply simple logic in an effort to ascertain the areas in which Thai public administration is most likely to need foreign aid, and how such assistance can be used most effectively.

A systematic projection of the need for foreign assistance to public administration and of the plans for such assistance requires us first to understand the salient features of public administration and of foreign aid. Then we need to review past and current aid to determine the pattern of the assistance Thailand has thus far received. This knowledge, together with a projection of the general situation of the country at the time for which the public administration projection is being made, should suffice. It follows that Thais must then determine what they are going to be able to do for themselves; then, and only then, can they know what they will need foreign assistance to accomplish. Following this line of simple logic, we shall attempt a projection of Thailand's need for foreign aid to public administration in the 1980s.

## Nature of Foreign Aid and Public Administration

First let us examine the special characteristics of public administration. When taken generally, it may mean merely the management of public affairs, but such a general meaning may cause serious misunderstanding as it includes a host of complexities which are only revealed when we ask ourselves "whose" affairs are being managed and how "public" those affairs are.

Public administration in this context must be thought of as the management of a country–in this case, Thailand. In this sense, public administration is an internal affair of a sovereign state, and consequently a very sensitive, "private" affair, indeed. The government of any country will be very cautious about having its public administration exposed to people outside its intimate administrative circles, let alone to foreigners. Moreover, public administration operates within a national culture—a product of the social and political evolution of the country. Therefore, principles and practices of public administration cannot easily be superimposed from outside. The science of public administration is a very soft science as it is value-laden; in fact, it is still more an art than a science. It is not easily transplanted. Transplants of many ideas, processes, and techniques from the West have been attempted in developing countries, but practically none of them are fully accepted into the national body politic. They rarely perform as effectively or viably as they do in their countries of origin.

The term "foreign aid" suggests that the recipient country is not self-sufficient in some particular areas which must be of interest to it; otherwise, outside aid would not be solicited. However, there are cases when help is not sought, but rather is suggested by the potential donor who "sells" the idea to the recipient country as something that it should have—in some cases it is even forced upon the receivers.

The objective of foreign aid is usually stated loftily as "an attempt to help others to better help themselves." That is, it is extended to make the receiving countries more self-sufficient so that they can stand on their own feet and be able to proceed on their own. After decades of foreign assistance, even the most optimistic observers can hardly overcome the impression that the donor countries have ulterior motives and are not acting solely from altruism. The most common observations are that donor countries seek partners in the cold war, or that they are helping themselves by establishing beachheads for economic, social, and political exploitation. Experts are sent to gather intelligence information or merely to find jobs for abundant manpower. Materials and equipment are sent to underdeveloped countries to help home industries sell their products or to get rid of outmoded models at exorbitant prices at the expense of the recipient who will have to pay for maintenance later on.

While some of these observations are overstated, the facts remain, at least in the area of public administration, that several facets of administration embrace sensitive security areas; that some experts are not fully competent for their assignments; and that some programs are not really necessary. There are also many programs which are too expensive for the poor recipient country to continue once the aid is terminated. And, many programs require the creation of new agencies which do not fit the general structure of the country, thereby causing trauma as the government tries to adjust to them.

To be truly helpful, foreign aid in the field of public administration must be a transaction between friendly countries with a long history of association, so that the security aspect will not become an issue and so that the long association may have produced a body of experts who really understand the country well enough to avoid their making impractical recommendations. Moreover, the recipient country itself must be very careful in accepting advice and must make sure that training is provided for its own people. In brief, a mutual interest must accompany foreign aid to public administration—a mutuality which all partners recognize and appreciate.

## Patterns of Past and Present Foreign Aid

As previously indicated, the terms "foreign aid" and "public administration" have their own distinctive meanings. In reviewing past aid programs to determine if clear patterns exist from which we may learn, and which may be used to help determine future patterns, unexpected difficulties arise. First and foremost, there is no precise definition of what is meant by "foreign aid to public administration." There is no definition of either term upon which parties in aid programs have agreed. While we could now construct such a definition, it would be of little assistance, since we have to use existing data as they have been categorized and compiled—such categorization and compilation implicitly assuming a definition, or definitions, that might, or might not, be compatible with the definition we could construct. Second, it is very difficult, if not impossible, to obtain reliable data for the years prior to 1955. The following account therefore relates primarily to the period since 1955; references to events occurring before 1955 being based largely upon personal recollections.

### *Foreign Aid, 1955-1966*

Foreign aid in the area of public administration did not begin until the 1950s, when the U.S. International Cooperation Administration (ICA—the predecessor of the U.S. Agency for International Development) somewhat belatedly began to realize that assistance programs (under the Truman Point Four Program, the Marshall Plan, and other later plans) were not going to be successful if there were no corresponding change in the organization and management of the governmental structures of the recipient countries. The ICA then created technical assistance programs in public administration in various allied countries—first in Turkey and the Philippines, and then in some of the Latin American countries.

In Thailand, foreign aid to public administration began in 1955 when the ICA agreed to help create the Institute of Public Administration (IPA) at Thammasat University. The IPA had three major components: a program of graduate studies leading to the degree of Master of Public Administration, an in-service training program for public officials throughout the government, and a research program. In the period of 1955-1964, the American contribution amounted to approximately 2 million dollars; forty-one Thais were sent to the U.S. for training, and forty staff members from Indiana University came to work for the IPA.[a]

[a]For further information, see the booklet *In Commemoration of the Termination of the Nine-Year Association in Public Administration between Thammasat and Indiana Universities, and the Governments of Thailand and the United States*, (October 8, 1964).

The U.S. also helped to improve the administration capabilities of the Ministry of Finance—mainly by improving the budgetary process and by Operations and Management studies which resulted in the creation of the modern Bureau of the Budget in the Office of the Prime Minister.

Another key area of U.S. assistance aimed at the improvement of provincial and city administration. The initial emphasis was on the Department of the Interior with the goal of improving *changwad* (province) and *ampur* (district) administrations through the O&M process. The effort then branched out to cover the in-service training program of the renamed Department of Local Affairs, which finally resulted in the creation of the Division of Training and the establishment of the Nai Ampur Academy—an administrative academy with a university-like structure. The effort to improve rural conditions led to the creation of the Department of Community Development of the Office of Accelerated Rural Development (ARD), and to the establishment of provincial organizations and other semilocal governmental units. (Assistance to the city of Bangkok, despite its benefits, also fed the city's excessive growth rate and urban sprawl.)

Since 1960, USAID has assisted the Civil Service Commission in the area of personnel administration—in devising a position classification system and new examination and recruitment processes.

The U.N., the Colombo Plan, and other individual countries have also provided help during this period, but their assistance was less extensive than that of the U.S.

## *Foreign Aid, 1967-1973*

Data concerning total foreign aid to Thailand have been compiled by the Department of Technical and Economic Cooperation (DTEC) by sector, by donor, by type, and by program.[b]

Data relating to the "administration" sector (Table 4-2) are broadly designed to cover the work of several agencies primarily in the Ministry of the Interior, the National Economic Development Board, and in other programs clearly seen as related to administrative improvement. However, data relating to several programs aimed at improving the administration and conditions of people in rural areas are included in the figures shown for the "community development" sector. Similarly, a number of programs related to improvement of the police function and classified as "public safety" include assistance to Departments of Police, Public Welfare, Community Development, the ARD Office, and many other departments that may be considered public administration. On the other hand, not all assistance listed in the administration sector is devoted to actual public administration activity.

[b]The author is grateful for the kind assistance rendered by several officials of DTEC Technical Services Division in gathering and analyzing the data presented herein.

Despite such difficulties, the statistics presented in Tables 4-1 to 4-4 and in those following the discussion give some idea of Thailand's dependence on foreign assistance (currently approximately 15 percent of the annual budget outlay).

Table 4-1 and 4-2 indicate total grant assistance to Thailand in 1973 and show how sources, types, and sectors are classified by DTEC. Tables 4-5 through 4-14 contain more detail for the year 1972, for which statistics are more fully available. Table 4-3 indicates technical assistance in the field of administration, as defined by DTEC, for the years 1967-1973. It shows the historical development and changes of composition of aid from various sources. Table 4-4 shows the types of assistance received in the year 1973 from various sources.

It is interesting to review some of the items listed by DTEC as comprising the "administration" sector. The list of projects in administration includes items such as local government administration, civil service improvement, management improvement of the Budget Bureau, local government in-service training, Labor Department Administration, statistical services, cadastral surveys for the Land Department, vehicle testing, local government financing, commodity and property management, customs improvement, regional planning, traffic study for the metropolitan area, multipurpose cooperatives, Thai-Israel rural development, primary products (for the Ministry of Commerce), English Language Center, and many others.

On the other hand, under the community and rural development sector, the following items are included among others: provincial water supply, improvement of the Memorial Bridge, ARD mechanical centers, social welfare, social development, family social work, hill tribe welfare, crop replacement and community development in the Northern highlands, national service for technical skill promotion, vocational training planning, vocational rehabilitation, self-help land settlements, and Thai-Australian rural development center.

The public safety sector includes USAID assistance to the Department of Police, which between 1966-1973 amounted to $72,984,185 plus *baht* 936,590,951 counterpart funds paid by the Thai government, thus totaling approximately 2,500 million *baht*. Many aspects of this assistance may be regarded as improvement of police administration.

From available data, much of which is presented in this paper, we can draw some conclusions. First, the pattern of aid has changed from major improvement in basic administration in the early years to more small programs and "non-projects" (piecemeal assistance to a large number of individual functional departments). Second, most of the aid in the administration sector consists of expert services. The second largest amount goes to fellowship training abroad, while the amount spent for equipment is only about 12 percent (this pattern is consistent with other data not presented herein). This pattern indicates that the donors finally take back most of their money. Third, by going through the list of projects compiled at DTEC, it is evident that Thailand has no systematic approach in its requests for foreign aid in the administration sector as well as in

**Table 4-1**
**Total Grant Assistance to Thailand by Source and Type, 1973 (Thousand U.S. Dollars)**

| Source | *Type:* Experts | Fellowships | Equipment | Other[b] | Total | Distribution (%) |
|---|---|---|---|---|---|---|
| U.S. AID[a] | 3,974 | 2,072 | 6,440 | – | 12,486 | 40.3 |
| U.N.[c] | 2,707 | 745 | 567 | 251 | 4,270 | 13.8 |
| Colombo Plan | 2,315 | 746 | 2,223 | – | 5,284 | 17.1 |
| Other Countries | 2,214 | 1,688 | 829 | – | 4,731 | 15.2 |
| Volunteer | 4,183 | – | – | – | 4,183 | 13.6 |
| Total | 15,393 | 5,251 | 10,059 | 251 | 30,954 | 100.0 |
| Distribution | 49.7 | 17.0 | 32.5 | 0.8 | 100.0 | |

[a]Including contract services.
[b]Consists of subcontracts, miscellaneous, executing & direct costs.
[c]Assistance from regional & interregional, regular program, UNDP/SIS.
Source: Technical Services Division, DTEC, April, 1974.

**Table 4-2**
**Grant Assistance by Sector and Source, 1973 (Thousand U.S. Dollars)**

| Sector | U.S. | U.N.[a] | Colombo Plan | Third Country | Volunteer | Total | Distribution (%) |
|---|---|---|---|---|---|---|---|
| Agriculture | 1,435 | 1,303 | 872 | 1,092 | 63 | 4,765 | 15.4 |
| Industry | 148 | 1,141 | 36 | 60 | 10 | 1,395 | 4.5 |
| Power | – | – | 168 | 187 | – | 355 | 1.2 |
| Commun | – | 110 | 2,033 | 48 | 19 | 2,210 | 7.1 |
| Health | 2,176 | 54 | 401 | 244 | 201 | 3,076 | 9.9 |
| Education | 185 | 882 | 1,158 | 2,436 | 3,426 | 8,087 | 26.1 |
| Community Dev | 2,693 | 487 | 199 | 189 | 359 | 3,927 | 12.7 |
| Administration | 678 | 208 | 417 | 385 | 7 | 1,695 | 5.5 |
| Public Safety | 4,760 | – | – | – | – | 4,760 | 15.4 |
| Service | – | – | – | – | 29 | 29 | 0.1 |
| Unclassified | 411 | 85 | – | 90 | 69 | 655 | 2.1 |
| Total | 12,486 | 4,270 | 5,284 | 4,731 | 4,183 | 30,954 | 100.0 |

[a]Assistance from regional and interregional, regular program, UNDP/SIS, and UNICEF not included.

Source: DTEC, 1974.

**Table 4-3**
**Technical Assistance by Source, 1967-1973 (Thousand U.S. Dollars)**

*Administration Sector*

| Year | U.S. | U.N. | Colombo Plan | Other Countries | Volunteer | Total | Distribution (%) |
|---|---|---|---|---|---|---|---|
| 1967 | 1,298.5 | 47.7 | 297.6 | 362.3 | 25.8 | 2,031.9 | 19.60 |
| 1968 | 959.0 | 78.0 | 326.4 | 360.0 | 2.0 | 1,725.4 | 16.63 |
| 1969 | 1,286.5 | 87.6 | 103.6 | 98.0 | 8.8 | 1,584.5 | 15.28 |
| 1970 | 298.5 | 42.0 | 189.5 | 283.4 | – | 813.4 | 7.84 |
| 1971 | 256.8 | 34.0 | 164.3 | 533.7 | – | 988.8 | 9.53 |
| 1972 | 537.0 | 608.6 | 138.1 | 249.0 | – | 1,532.7 | 14.78 |
| 1973 | 678.0 | 208.0[a] | 417.0 | 385.0 | 7.0 | 1,695.0 | 16.34 |
| Total | 5,314.3 | 1,105.9 | 1,636.5 | 2,271.4 | 43.6 | 10,371.7 | 100.00 |
| Distribution | 51.24 | 10.66 | 15.78 | 21.90 | 0.42 | 100.00 | |

[a]Assistance from regional and interregional, regular program, UNDP/SIS and UNICEF not included.

Source: DTEC, 1974.

**Table 4-4**
**Technical Assistance to Thailand by Type, 1973 (Thousand U.S. Dollars)**

*Administration Sector*

| | Experts | | | Fellowships | | | | |
|---|---|---|---|---|---|---|---|---|
| Source | No. | M/M | Value | No. | M/M | Value | Equipment | Total |
| U.S. AID | 11 | – | 390.1 | 37 | – | 212.5 | 75.5 | 678.1 |
| U.N. | 5 | 44 | 111.6 | 15 | 102 | 73.7 | 22.7 | 208.0 |
| Colombo Plan | 38 | 174 | 249.0 | 50 | 261 | 90.8 | 77.1 | 416.9 |
| Other Countries | 25 | 200 | 285.1 | 38 | 306 | 90.0 | 10.0 | 385.1 |
| Volunteer | 1 | 9 | 7.2 | – | – | – | – | 7.2 |
| Total | 79 | 427 | 1,043.0 | 140 | 669 | 467.0 | 185.3 | 1,695.3 |

the other sectors. Apparently sources of aid are approached by various agencies of the government with no policy guidance and no coordination. Similar items may be requested by various departments from different countries. If Thailand is to use foreign aid more effectively and rationally, aid policy must be much better coordinated from the Thai standpoint. Some suggestions toward this end will be discussed more fully later.

**Scenario for Thailand in the 1980s and Likely Governmental Reaction**

Though the 1980s are only a few years away, no one heretofore has constructed an outline, even intellectually, of what Thailand will be like. A number of Thais have tried to plan for the long-range survival of Thailand from the present up to the year 2000 and beyond, but they have not worked out a detailed conceptualization of Thailand in the mid-1980s. However, presented here is a general scenario of Thailand which the author has deduced from the report entitled "Utilization of Resources and Conservation of Environment: The Struggle for National Survival," issued by the group working on the year-2000 study. A similar extrapolation of current trends and conditions yields a projection of likely governmental reaction to the scenario.

*Scenario*

Thailand in 1985 is likely to have a population of approximately fifty-five million, an increase of fifteen million from 1973. This population will need, at the minimum, 10.4 million tons of paddy rice for home consumption. This will be about equal to total domestic production. Therefore, the cereal supply will be barely adequate for the populace, while other food supplies, especially protein, will be very short, as has been apparent since the early 1970s. The supply of fish will dwindle due to overcatching from the sea and to pollution of all waterways and the ocean. The arable land for cultivation, 90 million *rais*, will be too small for a population of fifty-five million and will not yield enough to feed the people. (The recommended standard is 2.5 *rai* per capita—or 137.5 million *rais* for fifty-five million people.) Therefore, great numbers of people are going to be very poor and may face mass starvation. All economic development projections show that the rich countries are going to be richer, and the poor poorer, even though in terms of per capita income the latter may earn more. The rising cost of all commodities is going to make goods too expensive for most people.

Resources in Thailand, especially mineral, will be depleted. Huge deposits of oil shale may be tapped, but at high cost. Forest reserves, estimated to be a mere 15 percent of the forests in 1973, will be further destroyed. Wood products, which have been major export items, will be exhausted by 1976, and importation will begin. With respect to energy, Thailand is likely to be in short supply. Oil reserves will be scarce. New energy sources such as the new "formula T. Eternal fuel," if they materialize, will help economically. Otherwise, Thailand will not have enough currency to buy the expensive crude oil that it will need from foreign countries.

The Bangkok metropolis is likely to grow beyond the 6 million mark by 1985. Other urban centers are likely to grow by 50 percent. Urban expansion is heightening the urgent need for heavy investment to provide basic services. Traffic and utilities problems are likely to become more acute. Industries in cities and outlying areas are going to spring up like mushrooms without adequately enforced zoning and pollution laws, thus making city living more hazardous. Pollution of the air and water, as well as noise and smell, is going to go far beyond safety points that had already been reached by the late 1960s. Health and sanitation will become the largest single problem for the urban population.

In rural Thailand most people will become poorer as land is further subdivided. Land tenancy will be greater. The prospect for land reform in accordance with the "land to the tillers" principle is dim, and we cannot expect such reform to be effective. Paradoxically, the number of large farms will be greater, paving the way for greater industrialization of agriculture. While this will help meet the problem of food shortages, it will also make the gap between rich farmers and poor peasants greater. The latter will be driven by competition and land grabbers to occupy public land which is mostly forest reserves. This in turn will create great political and environmental problems. Another large portion of the displaced peasantry will come to urban centers looking for jobs. As they are unskilled and rural in outlook, they will be the lowest paid among labor groups. Many of them are going to be unemployed or unemployable. They will increase labor unrest, crime, squatting, and slums in the cities.

In terms of security, Thailand in the 1980s is likely to face more violence. Terrorist activity and plain robbery are apt to increase, both in rural and urban areas. In fact, communist and other leftist movements are likely to move from rural to urban centers—especially to the capital—due to the weakening authority of the national government and easier infiltration from neighboring countries. The national government is more likely to fight back than to give up; therefore, much of the government's resources will be devoted to suppression of communist activity, instead of being committed to combating poverty and to promoting development.

This scenario, though very roughly sketched, provides a background which government planners must seriously take into account if any realistic and systematic planning is to be done.

*Public Administration in the 1980s*

What will be happening in the 1980s depends a great deal on external forces–especially international political forces over which Thailand does not have sufficient control. It will also depend on what Thailand can do between the mid-1970s and the end of the decade. Of course, a great deal can be done, depending on Thai objectives and stamina, yet half a decade is not much time in which to accomplish a great deal. If the present trend and policies continue, governmental administration during the next decade is likely to concentrate on problems arising in the following areas.

1. **National Security** will be a prime concern of the government, assuming that the present internal and external situations continue to develop along the present lines. Conventional armed forces will be maintained at current levels if not increased. Increased nonconventional forces will be deployed against insurgents. Border police and rural security forces of all types will require a large share of the government's resources.

2. **Social and Political Stability**, in both the provinces and the capital, will be maintained by a stronger police force if political unrest persists or poverty increases. This stronger force will be supported by the major agencies involved in the judicial process–namely, the Attorney General's Office, the Ministry of Justice, and the Department of Correction–agencies which are, at present, being asked to make costly reforms.

3. **Urban Development** will absorb more government attention and resources than at present, despite policy statements to the effect that rural development is a greater national concern. The Bangkok metropolis is likely to grow even faster than the present 5 percent annual increase of its population. The government will have to pay heavily to keep Bangkok liveable in terms of utilities, transportation, health, and education services. It might sink or get flooded due to overuse of underground water, and it will be heavily polluted–thus requiring great expenditures for maintenance or improvement of the city. Other cities in various regions will also be growing. They, too, will need great investment to make them modern enough to be able to attract rural migrants who otherwise will come to Bangkok. Cities will cost much more to develop than rural areas due to land prices, labor costs, and the more sophisticated services they need.

4. **Rural Development**, while less costly per capita, will take more government energy in terms of agencies and officials involved. This will be the concern of at least thirty departments which will send officials to the rural areas to do developmental work to assist in maintenance of law and order–which will grow into a more complex task as land tenancy, poverty, and poor health become

more prevalent. These agencies are likely to look for better ideas, and then try to obtain help from outside to implement the ideas.

5. **Resource Management** is a vast new field that the government will have to enter. In the past the nation's resources have been laid open to any exploiter who came and grabbed whatever he could, with little government interference except for the purpose of levying nominal excises. In fact, in Japanese and German literature, Thailand is referred to as a resource-rich country. Now such resources as arable land, forests, fisheries, and minerals are being depleted very rapidly. The government can no longer afford to sit idly by, waiting for exploiters. It must study the stock of Thai resources carefully and prepare plans to use them for the maximum benefit. Resource management is a mammoth task, and one to which the Thai bureaucracy has never geared itself, even mentally.

6. **Environmental Management** will be a necessary component of resource management, and of industrial and urban development. Thailand is already facing environmental problems of great magnitude. With its outmoded laws and corruptible officials, the problems will grow worse, forcing the government to perform better. Environmental management will require a combined knowledge of science, technology, and management. It will also call for a new attitude and insight on the part of the environmental managers—the zest to improve the quality of life of the Thai people and a very long-term vision of the future of Thailand and of the entire globe. These qualities will be hard to cultivate, and still harder to apply.

7. **Agricultural Management** will become a necessity as food shortages become acute. Already there are several agencies assigned to improve food production, but they have not been able to link up the entire system. Despite great technological development, the peasantry has very minimal knowledge and very little capital to buy machinery, fertilizer, and pesticides. Peasants simply do not have enough food and basic tools for each growing season. They have to borrow, but the interest charges are too high while the prices of their products are too low and uncertain. The outmoded legal system works in favor of the "bloody-faced land-mongers." Export markets and prices are very uncertain and do not correspond to annual forecasts. Links between the knowledge of meteorology, hydrology, agricultural sciences, agronomy, and home economics do not exist, let alone support interactions in practice. All these factors will have to be changed if food production, as well as conditions of the peasantry, are to be improved.

8. **Management of the Economy** will become more imperative. At present, private business is too frequently run by non-Thais to the disadvantage of Thais.

On the other hand, public agencies are actually working in favor of businessmen and industrialists at the expense of Thai consumers and laborers. Public enterprises are well known for inefficiency and indifference to public needs. These facets of the national economy will have to be changed if resources are going to be mobilized for the maximum benefit of the Thais, not foreign exploiters. Industrial and agricultural products should be controlled in terms of quality, quantity, and price. Consumers and original producers of raw material and agricultural products should be protected. Banking and financial institutions must be controlled or at least supervised closely so that the few who control these institutions will no longer strangle the people in other sectors of the economy. Given the strange economic power composition in Thailand, in which foreigners are given choice advantages over the natives, perhaps the most enlightened alternative is more manipulation of the economy in terms of prices and wages. In this regard, Thai bureaucracy will have to change its outlook and orientation. The concept of Western capitalism will have to be reviewed; its institutions, which Thais have borrowed, dismantled. New views and new institutions will have to be built.

9. **Social Service Administration** will be expanded in all directions. First, population planning and control will have to be much more extensive to reach even the most reluctant villagers; otherwise, the population explosion will not be contained appreciably. Preschool children will need more attention from the government. Free nutritious food will have to be distributed to these children; otherwise, their health and mental development will be irrevocably impaired. Educational facilities must be extended both vertically and horizontally. At the moment, the government is able to provide four years of free schooling almost universally, but the attempt to extend free schooling to seven years is already becoming a great strain. Universal education of sixteen years is being suggested without any possible way to finance it. Increased health services are also being demanded by the public, yet public hospitals are inadequate; promotive, preventive, and rehabilitative measures are even worse. Social welfare services for the young, the old, the handicapped, and for women are also called for. Labor welfare benefits pose a separate set of problems. All these services have been ineffective and inadequate. A great deal of talent and resources will be required to make them less so. In this situation administrative machinery will need extensive overhauling before it can be expected to meet the challenge properly.

The problems outlined constitute the areas of greatest need and demand in order of priority, to which the Thai government in the 1980s is likely to respond, the author's personal preference notwithstanding. Preferably, the first five priorities should be reversed. Without proper management of resources, the country will face very difficult problems immediately as well as in the years ahead. National security and social order are necessary priorities for any government, but there should be alternatives to the use of force and coercion, if for no other reason than that the latter would require extensive material support.

On the other hand, we can look at these problem areas from another angle. To increase services in all these areas, there are common administrative elements the government has to provide, either from its own resources or from external aid. These elements are adequate, competent, well-trained, and properly motivated manpower; adequate financial and material support; the necessary technical know-how, methodologies, and equipment; efficient administrative arrangements including planning, coordination, control, and evaluation.

Judging from its experience and available resources, the Thai government cannot solve these problems alone. During the past several decades, all kinds of aid have been solicited and obtained from various countries and organizations. Since all problems seem to grow more complex and extensive while available resources do not grow proportionately (in some areas they may be dwindling), the Thai government in all probability will have to seek more help from outside. This may not sound complimentary to Thailand, but these observations are based on the following assumptions: First, it is assumed that Thailand will face more armed insurrection, both from internal and external sources; insurrection will thus cost the government so heavily that there will be inadequate resources left for sustenance and development of the country. Second, it is assumed that international détente will not be achieved to the extent that Thailand's integrity is fully safeguarded against foreign intervention. Third, internal economic forces will continue to serve the narrow interests of pariah entrepreneurs and industrialists at the expense of the Thai consumers and producers, thereby widening the gap between the rich and poor. Fourth, natural resources will be used selfishly. Fifth, the bureaucracy will continue to be inefficient, corruption-prone, and self-serving.

The greater the extent to which these assumptions are operative in the 1980s, the more likely it is that the Thai government will have to increase its dependence on outside assistance to keep the country going. Conversely, to the extent that these assumptions are less accurate, the more self-sufficient Thailand will be. While it is true that no government would like to rest its survival on the mercy of other countries, it is also true that in the modern world interdependence is unavoidable. Furthermore, the term "aid," as used in this paper, is meant to be very broad. No country is expected to stand alone without loans, bilateral and multilateral agreements, trade and credit deficits to some countries, nor, for that matter, without interchange of ideas and technological borrowing.

## Foreign Aid for the 1980s

As Thailand is facing certain poverty, and political and social turmoil are highly probable, foreign aid (especially multilateral loans at concessional rates) is certain to be required, at least at the current level of approximately 15 percent of the government's annual budget. We have already dealt with the alternatives for arranging priorities among the various areas of administration. Which are the high priority areas depends on the nature of the threat to national security and how the government decides to cope with it. If the government decides to use force against insurgencies, the priority areas will be as described earlier. But if there is no insurgence, or if the government decides to use other means to contain it, then the priorities may be switched. If national survival and continuing prosperity are the aims, then resource management, rural development, urban development, environmental management, and agricultural management in the various sectors of the economy must receive highest priority.

Regardless of the policy pursued by the future government of the 1980s, the nine areas indicated are the ones that will probably need foreign assistance to augment Thailand's own resources, since (despite the lofty ideals espoused by some intellectuals) present resources and the orientation of Thai officials are still inadequate—materially and psychologically, respectively.

To deal rationally with the situation of the 1980s, the government should develop strategies to maximize the benefit from foreign aid and loans in the area of public administration. The steps that should be taken include the following.

1. *Developing an integrated policy for assistance in public administration* should be a primary consideration. In the past, foreign aid in this area has not been guided by any clear policy. Agencies have been left almost entirely to themselves in seeking outside assistance. For the 1980s the government should at least develop a policy that foreign aid should be sought for the purpose of improving administrative efficiency through new knowledge, new methods, and new equipment rather than through extensive use of foreign experts—especially in sectors closely associated with national security. Foreign aid should not be used by Thai agencies to promote the adoption of procedures foreign to our system of administration, especially procedures which grow beyond our means to sustain later on. To implement this policy, a new advisory committee on aid to public administration should be created to supersede the old but ineffective mechanism of the DTEC; or, as proposed below, a national planning agency should be created and armed with the authority to review aid proposals initiated by the agencies.

2. *Strengthening staff agencies* at continuing levels so as to permit them to maintain this strengthened position should be given high priority. Such action is far preferable to scattering aid resources among a number of operating agencies. The Bureau of the Budget, the Civil Service Commission, the National Economic and Social Development Board, the National Statistical Office, and the National Research Council are among the key staff agencies for Thailand. They need continuing support so that they can keep abreast of modern technology, processes, and equipment. A National Policy Development and Planning Office should be created as the principal policy formation and development agency for

the entire government. The new science of policy development should be imported to Thailand. These staff agencies, once they have obtained modern know-how, should be encouraged to offer training programs in areas of their competence to other agencies. In this way new knowledge will spread at less cost than by letting each agency seek to secure such knowledge on its own from various countries without consideration of its propriety and suitability to the Thai environment.

3. *Strengthening existing academic and training institutions* by providing continuing support—such as equipment, fellowships, and internships in foreign countries—should also be given high priority until the much heralded promises to strengthen them with internal resources are actually realized. This is of the utmost importance if Thailand is to develop its own corps of competent people in adequate quantity. In the past a number of schools and institutes have been established with outside help and have been vigorous for a few years. However, when the aid phases out and stops, they lose their effectiveness. Such institutions need continual additional inputs of resources if they are to be effective. The government in the past has not given them enough resources to grow on their own and has not given them enough recognition by relying on them for expert advice and technical manpower even though many institutes are fully capable now of providing such assistance. An increased use of internal expert advisors would not only benefit the country in many ways, but would also increase the competence of such advisors in dealing with the practical problems of the society.

4. *Foreign technology, processes, and equipment* are more important to Thai agencies than experts and advisors. Experts and advisors who come to Thailand are usually not of high quality. The best people are used at home. Moreover, they may give the wrong advice because of an inadequate understanding of the country. They also cost more than would Thai advisors. It would be of great help if the donor countries were willing, when giving equipment and the necessary knowledge to operate it, also to set up specific operating funds to ensure that the work will go on. One big weakness of the Thai government is its willingness to create an agency, give it a building, allocate to it superfluous personnel, salaries and benefits, but then fail to grant it adequate operating expenses, thereby hampering the use of the support that has been provided by the imposition of stringent and unsympathetic controls that make it impossible to spend any money made available sensibly. Every agency is short of cash, and it tries to do a better job by seeking foreign assistance—a wrong solution to the right problem.

5. *Fellowships* as an aspect of foreign aid programs should be used more effectively. Usually Thais are anxious to go abroad to study for academic degrees. Fellowships for such study are overused in many agencies as an incentive to lure people to work. Often the fellowship recipient has no particular interest in the type of work done by the agency from which he has received his

fellowship. But the practice continues. Actually, agencies need people who are dedicated to the line of work they really like. These people have to be well trained, which includes periodic retraining. Therefore internships, inspection tours, short training courses, and the like, will often be of greater benefit to the agencies than sending people to colleges and universities. Thus foreign aid should be concentrated more on training than on studying. Meanwhile, the Thai government must give greater credit to the performance of people than to their paper credentials, and reward them accordingly.

6. *Equipment* needs should be scrutinized much more carefully. In the past, much of the equipment received has been either too outmoded or too advanced. Thailand, being a poor country, cannot afford expensive maintenance; therefore, equipment received should be standardized, easily repairable, and durable. Too large a variety of models and luxury items should be avoided for the same reasons.

These strategies, while rational enough, are likely to run counter to the wishes of the donors as well as those of the requesting agencies, though for different reasons. Donor countries and organizations are likely to prefer to send experts rather than train Thais; to prefer to send outmoded, complicated equipment rather than more durable and more easily maintained equipment. The agencies, on the other hand, like to have experts around to impress people, and to have luxurious equipment to enhance their prestige. The agencies are not likely to entertain the idea that staff agencies are more strategically placed than operating agencies. Thus the strategies recommended here must be implemented by the government, which in fact means by a few responsible persons and agencies; otherwise, the old pattern will continue to dominate the foreign aid scene in the 1980s and this paper will be worthless.

The advisory committee to coordinate foreign aid programs, as proposed herein, should be created as soon as possible if the existing committees cannot be made truly effective. It should work closely with the NESDB as the latter prepares the fourth five-year plan. Moreover, the committee should seek the advice of the Council of Administrative Advisors to the Prime Minister, which has been following the performance of most agencies for nearly two decades. The Council is in a position to inform the Committee about weak areas of management that really need improvement.

# Discussion: The Amara Paper

Amara began his discussion of his paper by noting that his approach was to make an estimate of Thailand's situation in the 1980s and then to ask what Thailand should be doing and what aid donors could be doing at that time. As stated above, Amara defended his scenario as a realistic set of predictions of Thailand's near future. Given the conditions projected, he believes priorities in public administration will be as set forth in his paper. Amara noted that these priorities do not reflect his preferences—he would very much like to see the first five reversed—but they are most likely to be as he ordered them in the paper. The future of Thailand depends fundamentally on whether force is used to suppress insurgency or whether other means are found for this purpose and higher priority is given to social reform.

Despite difficulties in adequately defining "public administration," there will be a need to work out strategies for development of public administration. Amara predicted that the six strategies posed in his paper will be objectionable to both Thai government and donor agencies; but, he concluded, "if we don't calculate and we don't think, Thailand will continue to develop in its own crazy way."

Seminar discussion of Amara's paper began with the criticism that the future he predicted in his scenario was perhaps too predetermined by the assumption of no change in current patterns of development or policy. In particular, in his discussion of public administration in the area of national security, Amara considered only military and police forces, the courts and the penal system, with no discussion of means other than force that might have been introduced before the 1980s to deal with domestic insurgency. Further, a second participant added, the scenario did not come to realistic grips with how the insurgency problem would and indeed could be addressed in an era in which U.S. aid to the Thai military and police forces would have declined drastically.

Amara sought to make clear the distinction between a projection and a prediction and replied that he fully agreed that policies other than reliance on force ought to be employed in the domestic security area, but, in his words, "maybe facing the future is facing the facts."

Several other portions of Amara's paper stimulated animated discussion and questions, not all of which implied acceptance of the distinction he had attempted to draw between a projection of current trends and conditions on the one hand, and a prediction based, in part, on conjectural variables and changes not a part of the base from which he departed, on the other hand. Some doubt was expressed as to whether Thailand ought to be seeking foreign aid in the 1980s in connection with the six objectives spelled out in the final section of the paper, or whether it would not be better for the nation to be making substantial efforts now to have achieved self-reliance in these respects by the 1980s. Amara responded that he did not envisage development as leading to self-reliance so much as to an interchange of technology and knowledge, with Thailand some day exporting as well as importing technical information and know-how.

It was pointed out that civil servants must reorient themselves in an era of political freedom and new demands on the civil service. It is no longer enough to know where roads should be built and how to manage their construction. Foreign aid might be used to train civil servants in new and more effective ways of dealing with people and to develop the capacity for independent action, if such training is available anywhere in the world.

One of Amara's proposals that stimulated debate was that the present unsystematic approach to aid policy coordination and guidance be corrected through the establishment of an advisory committee. It was noted that several such committees already exist; and the speaker then added rather caustically that conferences are notorious for recommending establishment of committees to solve even the most difficult and complex problems, and that this is hardly helpful in a system already overloaded with committees, subcommittees, and working groups that duplicate and overlap each other. A participant from an international aid agency praised Thailand's Department of Technical and Economic Cooperation (DTEC), noting that coordination of foreign aid in Thailand has been used by his organization as a model for other countries.

Finally, in response to Amara's observation on the low level of competence of many foreign advisors, participants emphasized the cost and difficulty of inducing qualified people to accept advisory assignments. Serious problems in coordinating technical assistance and in assuring proper use of foreign advisors, no matter how well qualified, were also noted.

Amara's analysis and evaluation were supported by the statistical tables presented in the following pages.

**Table 4-5**
**Total Grant Assistance to Thailand by Source and Type, 1972 (U.S. Dollars)**

DTEC–1/10

| *Type:* Source | Experts | Fellowships | Equipment | Other[a] | Total | Distri-bution (%) |
|---|---|---|---|---|---|---|
| U.S. AID | 6,557,215.00 | 2,322,620.00 | 7,560,820.00 | – | 16,440,655.00 | 43.5 |
| U.N. | 3,762,218.00 | 938,185.00 | 1,571,282.00 | 268,285.00 | 6,539,970.00 | 17.3 |
| Colombo Plan | 2,303,548.00 | 592,805.00 | 2,363,617.00 | – | 5,250,970.00 | 14.0 |
| Other Countries | 2,654,009.75 | 1,437,716.25 | 907,982.17 | – | 4,999,708.17 | 13.2 |
| Volunteers | 4,556,000.00 | – | – | – | 4,556,000.00 | 12.0 |
| Total | 19,832,990.75 | 5,291,326.25 | 12,403,701.17 | 268,285.00 | 37,796,303.17 | 100.0 |
| (%) | 52.4 | 14.0 | 32.9 | 0.7 | 100 | |

[a]Composed of subcontracts and miscellaneous components.

Source: Technical Services Division, Department of Technical and Economic Cooperation, 1973.

**Table 4-6**
**Grant Assistance by Sector and Source, 1972 (U.S. Dollars)**

DTEC–2/10

| Sector | U.S. | U.N. | Colombo Plan | Third Countries | Volunteers | Total | Distribution (%) |
|---|---|---|---|---|---|---|---|
| Agriculture | 2,029,960.00 | 1,958,900.00 | 904,020.00 | 1,136,158.72 | 96,000.00 | 6,125,038.72 | 16.2 |
| Industry | 474,235.00 | 621,950.00 | 47,765.00 | 142,205.00 | – | 1,286,155.00 | 3.4 |
| Power | – | 45,050.00 | 178,946.50 | 188,762.05 | – | 412,758.55 | 1.1 |
| Commun | – | 258,490.00 | 2,471,878.75 | 121,167.18 | – | 2,851,535.93 | 7.6 |
| Health | 2,270,586.00 | 1,178,450.00 | 285,014.50 | 118,094.35 | 316,800.00 | 4,168,944.85 | 11.0 |
| Education | 368,800.00 | 1,160,210.00 | 716,959.50 | 2,563,487.79 | 3,710,000.00 | 8,519,457.29 | 22.5 |
| Community & Soc Dev | 3,879,400.00 | 708,347.00 | 456,081.25 | 209,009.33 | 318,000.00 | 5,570,837.58 | 14.7 |
| Administration | 537,000.00 | 608,573.00 | 138,096.00 | 248,954.75 | – | 1,532,623.75 | 4.1 |
| Public Safety | 4,805,685.00 | – | – | – | – | 4,805,685.00 | 12.7 |
| Unclassified | 2,074,989.00 | – | 61,208.50 | 271,869.00 | 115,200.00 | 2,523,266.50 | 6.7 |
| Total | 16,440,655.00 | 6,539,970.00 | 5,259,970.00 | 4,999,708.17 | 4,556,000.00 | 37,796,303.17 | 100.0 |
| (%) | 43.5 | 17.3 | 14.0 | 13.2 | 12.0 | 100.0 | |

Source: Technical Services Division, Department of Technical and Economic Cooperation, 1973.

**Table 4-7**
**U.S. Program Assistance by Sector, 1972 (U.S. Dollars)**

DTEC–3/10

| Sector | Experts | | Fellowships | | | Equipment | Total |
|---|---|---|---|---|---|---|---|
| | No. | Value | U.S. | Other | Value | | |
| Agriculture | 32 | 715,380 | 81 | 52 | 522,910 | 791,670 | 2,029,960 |
| Industry | 9 | 269,000 | 25 | 3 | 205,235 | – | 474,235 |
| Commun | – | – | – | – | – | – | – |
| Health | 15 | 409,000 | 39 | 53 | 381,846 | 1,479,740 | 2,270,586 |
| Education | 16 | 329,000 | 2 | 6 | 39,800 | – | 368,800 |
| Community & Soc Dev | 147 | 1,545,000 | 50 | 61 | 404,300 | 1,930,100 | 3,879,400 |
| Administration | 19 | 418,000 | 14 | – | 117,900 | 1,100 | 537,000 |
| Public Safety | 40 | 1,420,000 | 41 | – | 127,475 | 3,258,210 | 4,805,685 |
| Unclassified | 62 | 1,451,835 | 41 | 39 | 523,154 | 100,000 | 2,074,989 |
| Total | 340 | 6,557,215 | 293 | 214 | 2,322,620 | 7,560,820 | 16,440,655 |

Source: Technical Services Division, Department of Technical and Economic Cooperation, 1973.

**Table 4-8**
**U.N. Assistance by Program, 1972 (U.S. Dollars)**

DTEC–4/10

| Program | Experts | | | Fellowships | | | Equipment | Other[a] | Total |
|---|---|---|---|---|---|---|---|---|---|
| | No. | M/M | Value | No. | M/M | Value | | | |
| UNDP | 209 | 1,406 | 3,552,618 | 235 | 1,615 | 838,985 | 628,282 | 226,555 | 5,246,440 |
| Regional & Interregional | 1 | 7 | 16,000 | 14 | 38 | 27,450 | – | – | 43,450 |
| Regular Programs | 11 | 45 | 116,100 | 17 | 125 | 71,750 | – | – | 187,850 |
| UNDP/SIS | 6 | 23 | 77,500 | – | – | – | – | 41,730 | 119,230 |
| UNICEF | – | – | – | – | – | – | 943,000 | – | 943,000 |
| Total | 227 | 1,481 | 3,762,218 | 266 | 1,778 | 938,185 | 1,571,282 | 268,285 | 6,539,970 |

[a]Composed of Subcontracts and miscellaneous components.

Source: Technical Services Division, Department of Technical and Economic Cooperation, 1973.

**Table 4-9**
**U.N. Assistance by Sector, 1972 (U.S. Dollars)**

DTEC–5/10

| Sector | Experts | | | Fellowships | | | Equipment | Other[a] | Total |
|---|---|---|---|---|---|---|---|---|---|
| | No | M/M | Value | No | M/M | Value | | | |
| Agriculture | 75 | 517 | 1,434,000 | 61 | 449 | 236,050 | 128,550 | 160,300 | 1,958,900 |
| Industry | 29 | 203 | 432,770 | 69 | 368 | 136,950 | 10,500 | 41,730 | 621,950 |
| Power | 2 | 16 | 40,000 | 1 | 9 | 5,050 | – | – | 45,050 |
| Commun | 11 | 56 | 140,000 | 14 | 49 | 60,950 | 44,335 | 13,205 | 258,490 |
| Health | 25 | 164 | 344,500 | 26 | 198 | 105,400 | 707,050 | 21,500 | 1,178,450 |
| Education | 46 | 245 | 613,600 | 54 | 501 | 271,260 | 243,800 | 31,550 | 1,160,210 |
| Community & Soc Dev | 14 | 135 | 307,500 | 5 | 12 | 8,800 | 392,047 | – | 708,347 |
| Administration | 25 | 145 | 449,848 | 36 | 192 | 113,725 | 45,000 | – | 608,573 |
| Unclassified | – | – | – | – | – | – | – | – | – |
| Total | 227 | 1,481 | 3,762,218 | 266 | 1,778 | 938,185 | 1,571,282 | 268,285 | 6,539,970 |

[a]Composed of Subcontracts and miscellaneous components.

Source: Technical Services Division, Department of Technical and Economic Cooperation, 1973.

**Table 4-10**
**Colombo Plan Assistance by Country, 1972 (U.S. Dollars)**

DTEC–6/10

| | Experts | | | Fellowships | | | | |
|---|---|---|---|---|---|---|---|---|
| Country | No. | M/M | Value | No. | M/M | Value | Equipment | Total |
| Australia | 79 | 544 | 778,090.50 | 29 | 216 | 69,945.00 | 1,238,550.00 | 2,086,585.50 |
| Jap. | 154 | 615 | 879,192.25 | 107 | 613 | 199,334.50 | 1,087,275.00 | 2,165,783.75 |
| U.K. | 60 | 311 | 445,490.75 | 60 | 1,122 | 273,037.50 | 29,827.00 | 748,355.25 |
| New Zealand | 16 | 106 | 151,831.25 | 10 | 110 | 29,710.00 | 7,983.00 | 189,524.25 |
| Canada | 7 | 34 | 48,943.25 | 5 | 54 | 17,852.00 | – | 66,795.25 |
| India | – | – | – | 3 | 23 | 2,926.00 | – | 2,926.00 |
| Total | 316 | 1,611 | 2,303,548.00 | 214 | 2,138 | 592,805.00 | 2,363,617.00 | 5,259,970.00 |

Source: Technical Services Division, Department of Technical and Economic Cooperation, 1973.

**Table 4-11**
**Colombo Plan Assistance by Sector, 1972 (U.S. Dollars)**

DTEC–7/10

| Sector | Experts | | | Fellowships | | | Equipment | Total |
|---|---|---|---|---|---|---|---|---|
| | No. | M/M | Value | No. | M/M | Value | | |
| Agriculture | 66 | 331 | 472,999.000 | 31 | 243 | 70,887.00 | 360,134.00 | 904,020.00 |
| Industry | 2 | 12 | 17,862.50 | 16 | 88 | 29,902.50 | – | 47,765.00 |
| Power | 14 | 55 | 79,309.50 | 5 | 20 | 7,231.00 | 92,406.00 | 178,946.50 |
| Commun | 111 | 701 | 1,001,371.75 | 16 | 90 | 29,472.00 | 1,441,035.00 | 2,471,878.75 |
| Health | 21 | 64 | 92,170.50 | 13 | 77 | 25,581.00 | 167,263.00 | 285,014.50 |
| Education | 40 | 240 | 344,389.00 | 80 | 1,305 | 320,474.50 | 52,096.99 | 716,959.50 |
| Community & Soc Dev | 29 | 143 | 204,704.25 | 6 | 61 | 16,948.00 | 234,429.00 | 456,081.25 |
| Administration | 26 | 37 | 53,587.50 | 39 | 200 | 68,254.50 | 16,254.00 | 138,096.00 |
| Unclassified | 7 | 26 | 37,154.00 | 8 | 50 | 24,054.50 | – | 61,208.50 |
| Total | 316 | 1,611 | 2,303,548.00 | 214 | 2,138 | 592,805.00 | 2,363,617.00 | 5,259,970.00 |

Source: Technical Services Division, Department of Technical and Economic Cooperation, 1973.

**Table 4-12**
**Other Countries and Nongovernment Assistance by Sector, 1972 (U.S. Dollars)**

DTEC–8/10

| Sector | Experts | | | Fellowships | | | Equipment | Total |
|---|---|---|---|---|---|---|---|---|
| | No. | M/M | Value | No. | M/M | Value | | |
| Agriculture | 69 | 533 | 761,657.00 | 79 | 620 | 208,615.50 | 165,886.22 | 1,136,158.72 |
| Industry | 11 | 59 | 85,025.50 | 28 | 156 | 57,179.50 | – | 142,205.00 |
| Power | 13 | 93 | 133,611.50 | 15 | 94 | 39,256.00 | 15,894.55 | 188,762.05 |
| Commun | 9 | 74 | 105,746.00 | 8 | 56 | 14,495.00 | 926.18 | 121,167.18 |
| Health | – | – | – | 37 | 348 | 110,807.00 | 7,287.35 | 118,094.35 |
| Education | 91 | 854 | 1,221,080.50 | 277 | 2,466 | 694,925.00 | 647,482.29 | 2,563,487.79 |
| Community & Soc Dev | 7 | 67 | 96,814.75 | 20 | 117 | 41,689.00 | 70,505.58 | 209,009.33 |
| Administration | 6 | 41 | 59,303.00 | 68 | 484 | 189,651.75 | – | 428,954.75 |
| Unclassified | 13 | 133 | 190,771.50 | 17 | 444 | 81,097.50 | – | 271,869.00 |
| Total | 219 | 1,857 | 2,654,009.75 | 549 | 4,788 | 1,437,716.25 | 907,982.17 | 4,999,708.17 |

Source: Technical Services Division, Department of Technical and Economic Cooperation, 1973.

**Table 4-13**

**Other Countries and Nongovernment Assistance by Country, 1972 (U.S. Dollars)**

DTEC–9/10

| Country | Experts | | | Fellowships | | | Equipment | Total |
|---|---|---|---|---|---|---|---|---|
| | No. | M/M | Value | No. | M/M | Value | | |
| Ger. | 84 | 683 | 976,721.00 | 71 | 437 | 163,125.00 | 804,598.42 | 1,944,444.42 |
| France | 24 | 204 | 291,873.25 | 115 | 1,457 | 287,716.50 | 2,411.15 | 582,000.90 |
| Netherlands | 7 | 62 | 88,598.00 | 70 | 548 | 189,543.00 | – | 278,141.00 |
| Denmark | 18 | 168 | 240,786.50 | 15 | 149 | 52,038.00 | 82,192.93 | 375,017.43 |
| Austria | 9 | 71 | 102,173.50 | 12 | 99 | 22,781.00 | – | 124,954.50 |
| Israel | 1 | 7 | 10,003.00 | 9 | 55 | 16,900.75 | – | 26,903.75 |
| Belgium | – | – | – | 3 | 17 | 2,931.00 | – | 2,931.00 |
| Italy | – | – | – | 7 | 70 | 14,990.00 | – | 14,990.00 |
| Switzerland | – | – | – | 2 | 24 | 3,432.00 | – | 3,432.00 |
| Greece | – | – | – | 1 | 12 | 2,428.00 | – | 2,428.00 |
| Norway | – | – | – | 21 | 207 | 56,377.50 | – | 56,377.50 |
| Sweden | – | – | – | 2 | 20 | 6,760.00 | – | 6,760.00 |
| The Rep of China | 33 | 200 | 286,514.50 | 27 | 167 | 35,357.50 | 1,535.25 | 373,407.25 |
| The UAR | – | – | – | 2 | 8 | 1,760.00 | – | 1,760.00 |
| Foundations | 43 | 460 | 657,340.00 | 192 | 1,516 | 531,576.00 | 17,244.42 | 1,206,160.42 |
| Total | 219 | 1,857 | 2,654,009.75 | 549 | 4,788 | 1,437,716.25 | 907,982.17 | 4,999,708.17 |

Source: Technical Services Division, Department of Technical and Economic Cooperation, 1973.

**Table 4-14**
**Volunteers by Sector and Source, 1972 (U.S. Dollars)**

DTEC–10/10

| Sector | U.S. Peace Corps | | | GVS | | | CUSO | | | VSO | | | VSA | | | Total | | |
|---|---|---|---|---|---|---|---|---|---|---|---|---|---|---|---|---|---|---|
| | No. | M/M | Value | No. | M/M | Value | No. | M/M | Value | No. | M/M | Value | No. | M/M | Value | No. | M/M | Value |
| Agriculture | 7 | 84 | 67,200 | – | – | – | 1 | 12 | 28,800 | – | – | – | – | – | – | 8 | 96 | 96,000 |
| Health | 21 | 252 | 201,600 | 3 | 36 | 28,800 | 1 | 12 | 28,800 | 1 | 12 | 28,800 | 1 | 12 | 28,800 | 27 | 324 | 316,800 |
| Education | 200 | 2,249 | 1,799,200 | 28 | 299 | 239,200 | 45 | 429 | 1,030,800 | 22 | 216 | 518,400 | 5 | 51 | 122,400 | 300 | 3,244 | 3,710,000 |
| Community & Soc Dev | 17 | 204 | 163,200 | – | – | – | – | – | – | 5 | 22 | 54,000 | 4 | 42 | 100,800 | 26 | 268 | 318,000 |
| Unclassified | 3 | 36 | 28,800 | – | – | – | 2 | 24 | 57,600 | – | – | – | 1 | 12 | 28,800 | 6 | 72 | 115,200 |
| Total | 248 | 2,825 | 2,260,000 | 31 | 335 | 268,000 | 49 | 477 | 1,146,000 | 28 | 250 | 601,200 | 13 | 117 | 280,800 | 367 | 4,005 | 4,556,000 |

GVS: German Volunteer Service.
CUSO: Canadian University Service.
VSO: Volunteer Service Overseas.
VSA: Volunteer Service Agency.
Source: Technical Services Division, Department of Technical and Economic Cooperation, 1973.

# Sources of Aid and International Relations in the 1980s: A Summary of Somkiat Ariyaprucha's Paper

Somkiat's paper contained three major parts. He first discussed sources and terms of aid, reviewing Tables 4-15 and 4-16. He then examined the motives of donors, arguing that aid was often given to achieve political or even social objectives of the donor countries rather than to meet the genuine needs of the recipient. And finally, he sought to predict Thailand's role in future international affairs, in consideration of shifts in power relationships now taking place.

In discussing terms of aid, Somkiat noted that much of the assistance to Thailand from the U.S. and the Colombo Plan nations had been in the form of grants, requiring no repayment of interest or principal. But there are burdens even to grants, as Thailand is required to provide counterpart funds including some support for foreign experts, grants are frequently tied to purchases of goods from the donor country, and some of the grants-in-kind carry a continuing obligation to purchase spare parts from the donor. In general, loans carry terms that are quite unfavorable to Thailand when compared to the terms recommended by the Pearson Commission.[a]

Somkiat then analyzed the evident objectives of donor nations, particularly the U.S. and Japan. He noted that military aid from the U.S. has been enormous in comparison with technical nonmilitary assistance ever since the basic Thai-U.S. Economic Assistance Agreement of 1950. The motives, in Somkiat's opinion, are obvious enough. The Chinese Communist Party took control of the Chinese mainland in 1949, the Korean War broke out in 1950, and in 1952 the U.S. announced its policy of "containment" of communism. Under the then-popular domino theory, it was considered essential to preservation of political stability in the rest of Southeast Asia that the big Thai domino not topple to the communists; and so Thailand was crucial to the containment policy. From 1964 to 1970, military aid to Thailand was also conditioned by the U.S. strong desire for use of Thai facilities in prosecution of the Vietnam War. In the 1950s, the U.S. began giving some economic aid to Thailand in an effort to strengthen the domestic position of friendly regimes. Much of this economic aid has gone to improve the police forces. In recent years, with U.S. disengagement from Vietnam, aid has not only declined but is going in larger proportion to developmental projects. The U.S. has publicly professed a change in emphasis from political to social objectives. But Somkiat remains skeptical, noting that the social objectives may be those of the U.S. rather than Thailand. For reasons

[a]These terms include an interest rate of not more than 2 percent per annum, a maturity of 25 to 40 years, and a grace period of 7 to 10 years. See Lester P. Pearson, *Partners in Development: Report of the Commission on International Development* (New York: Praeger, 1969).

of domestic problems with drug addiction, the U.S. is making additional efforts to curb poppy growing in Thailand and other nations.

Japan, Somkiat continued, has an ambivalent attitude towards foreign aid. She is still in the process of finding her place in Asia, recognizing on the one hand her growing political and economic importance and the fact that her neighbors and trading partners in the region are developing nations. On the other hand, Japan still considers herself short of capital for domestic development, and until very recently was confining her assistance to loans and suppliers' credit on commercial terms. But in the face of growing Asian resentment, Japan is now softening the terms of her assistance. Further, Japan realizes that as time passes and the U.S. reduces its involvement in Asia, China will grow in importance to the rest of the region, and Japan will find herself more and more in competition with China for economic and political influence in Asia.

Somkiat then turned to his own scenario for Southeast Asian international affairs in the 1980s. By the mid-1980s he thinks the war in Vietnam will "probably" be settled and that détente between the U.S. and the Soviet Union will have grown to the point where U.S. political interests in Southeast Asia will be quite attenuated. The Russians are likely to increase their naval strength in the Indian Ocean, but the dominant forces both on the Asian mainland and in the Pacific will be Japan, China, and a nuclear-armed India. Somkiat shared Amara's pessimistic view that Thailand would still be troubled by internal guerrilla activities in the 1980s.

The realities of the fact that the major powers exerting their influences on Thailand will also be much closer geographically than was the case in the past means that neither Thailand nor the other relatively small Southeast Asian nations, even including Indonesia, will be able to pursue independent foreign policies based on assessments of their separate bargaining strengths or narrow national objectives. Rather, it is more likely that the Southeast Asian countries will recognize the need for a coalition, at least as far as international relations are concerned, and will move towards the establishment of a neutral bloc in the region.

A policy of neutrality in coordination with neighboring nations will clearly influence Thailand's aid strategy. She will no longer be able to depend on a single donor or accept aid based on the political considerations of any particular donor. Instead, there must be an ideological reorientation within the nation to put Thailand in a position to solicit and accept aid from sources that would enhance rather than jeopardize neutrality. This in turn implies much greater reliance on multinational donors.

Somkiat offered specific recommendations. Agreeing that trade can contribute more to development than aid, he pointed out that the developed countries have not been receptive to the efforts of Thailand and other developing countries in international negotiations to obtain more favorable trade conditions, particularly in regard to tariff and quota treatment of their exports.

He urged that aid not be tied to purchases from the donor, that terms of loans should be those recommended by the Pearson Commission, and that future aid should be given solely for purposes of the social and economic development of Thailand as formulated by Thais themselves rather than the donors. He closed by noting that he would particularly welcome the reactions of participants from the donor nations and organizations to his suggestions.

## Discussion: The Somkiat Paper

None of the participants questioned Somkiat's assessment of the political motivations of donors. And there was general acceptance of his predictions regarding changes in the international situation in the future. But a number of participants did respond to his invitation to comment on his specific suggestions.

Mr. Lucas agreed that trade was preferable to aid for purposes of pure and simple economic development, but he was not at all sure that this would be true for the kinds of social and political development being emphasized at the Seminar. He maintained that there was a need for reform of tax and other laws in Thailand to give an incentive to the growth of local philanthropies so that foreign foundations would be freer to concentrate on areas where foreign input would be most useful. This was of particular importance, Mr. Lucas continued, because while it may have been true that U.S. governmental aid to Thailand had been given primarily to serve the military and political objectives of the U.S., this was not the case for the American foundations.

Considering the significance of Thai neutrality in respect to future aid, Dr. Narongchai raised the question of the relative merits of bilateral and multilateral aid from the viewpoints of both recipients and donors. Much of the ensuing discussion grew out of his comment. The following were among the observations made. Multilateral and bilateral aid are not mutually exclusive options. There is room for cooperation among multilateral and bilateral donors. Multilateral donors have access to large resources but must lend on intermediate terms to obtain funds. Bilateral donors have smaller resources but can offer better terms. With the shift in emphasis from projects with calculable economic benefits to the use of aid for broader social development purposes, it may be hard to justify to domestic budgetary authorities the use of funds borrowed at fairly high rates of interest. The multilateral sources can resist political and other extraneous considerations, and often bilateral donors cannot do so. Funds given unilaterally to multilateral agencies can be lent on very favorable terms. Strong protest was lodged against Narongchai's comment that many viewed the multilateral agencies as inefficient. The U.N. is implementing the Jackson Report,[1] including a country approach and strengthening of the role of resident representatives. There will be a review in 1975 of the U.N. development strategy and hopefully goals will be redefined in such a way that Thailand can again subscribe to them. There are encouraging signs that bilateral donors are increasingly willing to provide aid through multilateral channels.

Mr. Blobel pointed out that one must keep in mind that the multilateral donors have no money of their own but rather must acquire funds from the affluent nations. Whether the funds are donated or the international agencies borrow on world markets, the agencies must depend on permission of the wealthier countries to enter their capital markets and to compete for their resources. Despite efforts by IBRD to get loan terms softened, cheap money will remain scarce. And it must be allocated. IBRD uses three criteria: poverty, effort, and creditworthiness. No soft loans will be made to nations with per capita incomes averaging over $300. Thailand meets this criterion, but the need is surely not as great as that of, say, Bangladesh, India, or Ethiopia. A recipient must demonstrate that it is making serious efforts to raise money internally and use aid effectively. This criterion inevitably involves the unpleasant matter of an external review of a nation's internal affairs, including tax collection efforts. And finally, a country seeking a low-cost loan must show that its debt burden is already so high that the low-cost loan is crucial to its development plan. Thailand's low-debt service ratio indicates that the nation could carry quite a bit more in the way of conventional debt.

It was suggested that bureaucracy and red tape might be avoided by providing aid directly to the private sectors which were expected to be the ultimate beneficiaries rather than channeling the funds through government agencies. This observation stimulated several comments about advantages and disadvantages of direct aid to private institutions—an issue which was also raised in connection with the paper by Drs. Sura and Twatchai. Difficulties were noted, including the problem that recipient governments would regard direct aid as gross interference in domestic affairs; the fact that it would be very hard for donors to identify appropriate areas and recipients in the private sector; and the inability of poorly organized, weak and often short-lived private organizations such as trade associations and farmers' associations to absorb and use loans or grants efficiently.

Somkiat replied to several of the comments. He saw serious problems in giving aid directly to the private sector when the government must assume the responsibility of determining development priorities. In regard to multilateral aid sources, he conceded that sometimes their sizes and constitutions contributed to inefficiency. But on the other hand, the multilateral organizations could draw on a world-wide pool of experts; and borrowing nations could feel that they were in a quite real sense drawing on their own funds in seeking assistance from multilateral organizations which numerous nations helped to support.

It was noted that there had been quite a bit of commentary on aid from the U.S. and Japan, but that other sources, such as the European Economic Community (EEC), had been neglected. The EEC countries taken together are the largest importer from Southeast Asia. In considering diversification of aid sources, it was suggested, Thailand ought to keep the EEC, the Soviet bloc and the Organization of Arab Petroleum Exporting Countries (OAPEC) in mind. OAPEC might soon be sending an economic mission to Southeast Asia, one participant reported.

In reply, Somkiat stated that he did not discuss EEC because EEC countries are already contributing aid through the Colombo Plan. EEC itself is a trade, not aid, bloc. OAPEC could be a major source of aid if the political will existed; but it is not clear that the terms would be favorable, and there is reason to be concerned that Arab aid might be politically oriented.

## Notes

1. Robert Jackson, *A Study of the Capacity of the United Nations Development System*, 2 vols. (Geneva: United Nations, 1969).

Table 4-15
**Aid to Thailand by Type and Source, 1967-1972**

| Source | Technical Assistance[1] 1967-1972 | Grant[2] 1972 only | As of December, 1973[3] | |
|---|---|---|---|---|
| | | | Direct Government Loans* | Guaranteed Loans* |
| U.S. | 214,387.4 | 16,440.7 | 65,904.0 | 45,750.0 |
| U.N. | 29,344.8 | 6,540.0 | – | – |
| Colombo | 28,559.1 | 5,251.0 | – | – |
| Jap. | 4,034.7 | – | 62,611.1 | 6,859.9 |
| U.K. | 4,972.3 | – | – | – |
| Australia | 13,277.1 | – | – | – |
| New Zealand | 4,226.4 | – | – | – |
| Canada | 2,048.6 | – | 994.1 | – |
| Ger. | 9,487.1 | – | 37,548.5 | 48,596.4 |
| France | 2,929.7 | 4,999.7 | – | 29,104.2 |
| Other Countries & Foundations | 13,846.3 | – | 3,581.7 | 9,832.0 |
| Volunteers | – | 4,556.0 | – | – |
| IBRD | – | – | 214,000.0 | 243,600.0 |
| ADB | – | – | 6,400.0 | 79,500.0 |
| Total | 298,554.4 | 37,787.4 | 391,039.4 | 463,242.5 |

Unit: Thousands of U.S. Dollars.
*Refer to the initial amount of contracted loans.
Sources: (1) DTEC, April, 1973. (2) Technical Services Division, DTEC, 1973. (3) Bank of Thailand.

**Table 4-16**
**Percentage Distribution of Aid to Thailand by Source and Type, 1972**

| Sources | Technical Assistance | Grant (1972 only) | Direct Government Loans | Guaranteed Loans |
|---|---|---|---|---|
| U.S. | 71.8 | 43.5 | 16.9 | 9.9 |
| U.N. | 9.8 | 17.3 | – | – |
| Colombo | 9.6 | 14.0 | – | – |
| Jap. | 1.4 | – | 16.0 | 1.5 |
| U.K. | 1.7 | – | – | – |
| Australia | 4.5 | – | – | – |
| New Zealand | 1.4 | – | – | – |
| Canada | 0.7 | – | 0.3 | – |
| Ger. | 3.2 | – | – | 10.5 |
| France | 1.0 | 12.0 | – | 6.3 |
| Other Countries & Foundations | 4.6 | – | 9.6 | 2.1 |
| Volunteers | – | 12.0 | – | – |
| IBRD | – | – | 54.7 | 52.6 |
| ADB | – | – | 1.6 | 17.2 |
| Total | 100.0 | 100.0 | 100.0 | 100.0 |

Source: Calculated from Table 4-15.

# 5 Project and Program Areas

*The Seminar did not concern itself entirely with such grand issues as past and future perspectives and the overall social and political contexts of foreign aid to Thailand. Four of the eight papers dealt with rather specific aspects of aid projects and programs. Dr. Ammar Siamwalla sought to assess the prospects for future foreign assistance in the development of rural Thailand. Dr. William A. McCleary reported on a study of road construction projects which was designed to shed light on the question of the relative social costs of capital-intensive and labor-intensive techniques of construction in a developing nation such as Thailand. Dr. Supachai Panitchpakdi addressed himself to the vital but extraordinarily difficult problems of giving effective aid to human and social development in the fields of education, population, and public health. And Drs. Sura Sanittanont and Twatchai Yongkittikul analyzed the effects of direct foreign investment on the Thai economy, recognizing that private investment from abroad can be viewed as a form of aid when it is encouraged, guaranteed, or subsidized by the governments of source countries.*

*Thoughtful and realistic analyses of the problems and prospects for various types of aid projects and programs were essential to relevant discussion of the issues facing the Seminar. The shift in focus of aid from the U.S., from a primarily politically oriented effort to a developmental one, has major implications, as noted by Ernst. Future U.S. aid should be quantitatively less significant than it has been in the past, but at the same time it and aid from other sources alike will demand more from the recipients in formulating proposed projects and programs and in implementing them effectively so as to assure that the benefits actually accrue to those whom the projects are designed to help. Similarly, Thai aspirations for social development leading to greater equity and justice as well as higher per capita income levels demand rigorous and hard-headed evaluation at the project and program levels.*

# Foreign Aid and Rural Development in the 1980s

**Ammar Siamwalla**

The subject of the role of foreign aid in rural development is a suitably vague one. When coupled with the phrase "in the 1980s," it becomes a license to be free of encumbrances that are known in scholarly or, perhaps more aptly, scholastic circles as "rigorous economics." This paper will therefore be an excursion into the trends of thinking on the subject of rural development, examining why such thinking (at least as traditionally conceived) leads to the natural conclusion that the role of foreign aid in this sort of activity will get smaller as time goes by.

Development economics has in the past treated the momentous issues that face it by means of stage theories, of which Rostow's is perhaps the best known recent instance.[1] It is therefore no more than poetic justice for us to turn around and apply this same technique to an interpretation of development economics itself.

Development economics has always been thought of as a program to understand and thus help solve the problems of income disparities between rich and poor. In its early childhood stage, the income gap that most people in the field were discussing was the gap between rich and poor *nations*. This was the period when GNP reigned supreme as the target of development and classic papers were written which dealt primarily with the issue of how to arrange (openly or stealthily), a flow of real resources from the richer to the poorer *nations* that would enhance most effectively the latter's GNP. The papers by McKinnon[2] and by Chenery and Strout[3] and the vast literature that grew up around the subject of the terms of trade between the industrialized and the nonindustrialized worlds are examples of the kinds of discussion that then took place. The discussions concerning the debt-servicing problem of the underdeveloped countries in the late 1960s may be regarded as a secondary wave, arising out of belated awareness of the burden of the original debts contracted in an earlier period when it was believed that foreign resources provided a painless answer to the problems of development.

But while these discussions were being carried on by economists, new techniques of analysis and measurement were being developed that began to focus on income disparities between *sectors* of the economy of an underdeveloped country. This is the second stage in the development of development economics. Of the various ways of sectoring the economy, the rural-urban contrast was chosen as the one that really matters. Two-sector models became the rage. One interesting feature of most such models is that they are largely closed-economy models, emphasis being placed on real resource flow between the two sectors that comprise the economy. International resource flows were, from the logic of the models, largely ignored, but it is not only logic that did foreign aid in. The facts themselves demanded that it be given only a minor role.

Aside from such dull things as logic and facts, there is a third factor which cannot be omitted, and that is politics. One does not need to be a Marxian to realize that any serious attempts to reduce income disparities within a given nation will alter the political balance within that nation. In such circumstances foreign aid would be seriously questioned (either by conservatives or radicals and not infrequently by both), as being biased in one way or another. We need not pause to examine whether such attacks are justifiable. We merely note one consequence: They have led (or provided the excuse for) donors to be more cautious in their aid programs than they would otherwise be.

As far as development economics is concerned, we are in the middle of this second stage. The very title of this paper reflects this frame of mind. Before I proceed to examine the more substantive issues involved, let me outline what I believe to be the next stage in the development of development economics.

The problem of development conceived of in terms of income disparities between two sectors (labeled "traditional and modern" or "rural and urban") has been shown to be seriously inadequate. That it is inadequate because it overlooks income disparities within the urban sector has long been realized. The tendency to lump the entire rural population together as a homogeneous aggregation of poor farmers has, however, also been very strong, and nowhere more so than in Thailand.[a] It is now slowly being recognized that measures to develop the rural sector will have to come to grips with the inequalities within that sector. The move from the first stage to the second increases the political complications: The move from the second to the third will compound them.

The preceding excursion into the history of thought was intended to provide the context for a discussion of the role of foreign aid and rural development in the 1980s. For if we are to believe Keynes' celebrated dictum,[4] the civil servants and the planners and the politicians of the 1980s will probably be following the trends and fashions of today's economists who will presumably by then be dead or defunct or both.

In this light, by the 1980s Thailand will be launched into the attempt, real or pretended, to lessen the wide disparities between the urban and rural sectors. What are the characteristics, or to use the hard language favored by foreign aid specialists, what is the "technology" of the activity we call "rural development"? It is only through understanding this clearly that we can derive the role of foreign aid.

Rural development means many things to many people. Building a modern

[a]The land tenure situation is a vast unknown in Thailand, not only with respect to the extent of tenancy, but also with respect to the identity of the landlords, who are usually lumped together (in the minds of land reformers) as "capitalists" without regard to whether these "capitalists" belong strictly to the "rural" or to the "urban" sector. By itself this distinction is unimportant, but it is important to the academic model-builder.

asphalt highway to a region previously inaccessible may be considered rural development by many. The same applies to the construction of irrigation systems. We may side-step the issue of whether this "really" constitutes rural development by pointing out that the "earlier" projects, which were undertaken first because they seemed to be the most promising in terms of their expected capital/output ratios, should be in place by the 1980s; and further investment of this kind, such as irrigation projects in the Northeast, would be extremely expensive, raising serious questions if any attempts were made to push further along this line. Highways and irrigation systems represent the types of activity that traditional modes of foreign aid are best equipped to handle, particularly when the aid is project-oriented as were the loans provided by IBRD which comprise a major component of Thailand's receipts from foreign aid.

Another type of inflow from abroad that will have a greater impact in the future is the inflow of technological know-how. If we adopt the Hayami-Ruttan approach to rural development problems,[5] we conclude that rural development is largely a matter of stimulating innovations, which may be thought of as either technological or institutional. I shall discuss institutional innovations later. For the moment let me examine the problem of technological innovations and the possible role of foreign aid in promoting them.

As I see it, there have been three major innovations that have led to an increase in total factor productivity in Thailand in the past. The first is the large-scale expansion of irrigation facilities which resulted from the large investments in infrastructure in an earlier period and the provision of ditches and dikes in many areas of the Central Plains in the last decade. The second is the introduction of nitrogen-responsive varieties of rice, which was probably the major factor explaining the expansion of dry-season cropping, particularly since 1969. The third factor is the substitution of mechanical for animal labor in ploughing. There may well be doubts concerning this third change or innovation, since it is not obvious that there has been a net increase in total factor productivity as a result. The introduction of new crops may be excluded because of even stronger doubts of the same nature.

Of these three innovations, irrigation expansion is associated with the type of large infrastructural investments that we have already touched upon. I shall concentrate on the second, as the role of foreign aid is of most relevance in this context.

The success of the set of innovations in rice production that goes by the name of "the Green Revolution" has been the result of a combination of the activities of an international research organization, the International Rice Research Institute (IRRI), financed from outside of Asia, and local research activities devoted to adapting the findings of IRRI to local conditions.

What the optimal combination between such international research and local research activities should be is an interesting question that should be further investigated. But whatever the results of such an investigation, there must surely be a place for the role of international research organizations of the type pioneered by IRRI.

As participants in this Seminar are all too well aware, what we have witnessed in the past two years or so has been a veritable price revolution which has led to a major displacement not only of the absolute price level, but also of the relative prices of the major inputs and outputs of Southeast Asian agriculture. Whether the future holds in store for us a stabilization of these prices or, instead, a price "counter-revolution" is a question everybody would like to have answered. Given this uncertainty, it becomes absolutely necessary for us to have several possible options for technological development. These several options can be provided only by international research organizations which can best afford to do the basic research, a necessary first step in providing us with those options.

Let me add a few final words on the role of international research organizations. I have advocated further aid in support of such organizations with the full knowledge that IRRI, particularly in the years 1969-1971, has been a source of external *diseconomies* to Thailand. I am nevertheless an optimist and still believe that technological progress in agriculture will be beneficial in the long run to all countries. Immiserizing growth is always a possibility, of course, but even its theoretical advocates are rather shy about its empirical relevance.

We come now to the first of the two most important of the problems of rural development, i.e., the problem of determining what institutional innovations are necessary to achieve a significant increase in rural incomes as a whole without at the same time increasing the income inequalities within the rural sector.

There is a widespread belief that *the* bottleneck to rural development is not any particular factor of production or the lack of technological know-how. The failure is believed to lie instead in the system of *delivery* of the factors or of the know-how. In some areas, this is immediately obvious–health care, for example. Modern knowledge concerning medicine and public health is readily available, sometimes in superabundance, but only in the urban areas. This knowledge is never transferred to rural areas. As another example, capital in underdeveloped countries is generally scarce, but financing the expansion of the urban sector has never posed much of a problem, particularly in the *private* sector within the urban areas. Given this presupposition, it is concluded that what is needed is the building of regular institutions that would facilitate the flow of the missing items from urban to rural areas. In some more ambitious schemes, these institutions are supposed to generate or mobilize the resources from within the rural sector itself; for example, cooperative credit societies. In any case, the common thread running through these institution-building schemes is the idea that the primary impetus should come from within the urban areas. This is because institution building requires some familiarity with modern organizational methods, at least in its initial stages. The rural sector is typically regarded as suffering from an absolute shortage of the type of personnel needed to initiate building up such institutions.

It is clear then that any attempts to build up rural institutions would be demanding, in terms of a particular kind of human resource that Schumpeter called "entrepreneurship." Since "entrepreneurs" are usually associated with capitalism, let us speak instead of "organizers." These organizers would have the job of setting up and running institutions whose main aim is to extract the available resources from urban areas. Given this, they would have to be very well versed in urban ways. In short, they have to be urban people themselves, particularly in the earlier stages. The availability of this class of people in sufficient numbers in the initial stages is what would determine the success or failure of the program of institution-building.

What role does foreign aid have to play in such institutional changes? If we look at the type of resources required, it seems that the best that can be achieved under the circumstances is that foreigners will, if anything, play merely a supportive role in subsidizing the flow of the organizers from urban to rural areas. The task of initiating, planning, and implementing such programs would necessarily be local.

Up to this point the problem of institutional innovation has been viewed as one of the most important problems in rural development. This problem tends to be emphasized by collectivist-minded thinkers over the second of the two most important problems affecting rural development, i.e., the distortions in the price system. But whatever one's ideological predilections, the conclusion for the role of foreign aid is the same, as I will now attempt to establish.

The price distortions mentioned above refer not only to the more obvious input and output prices such as fertilizer and rice prices, but also to a whole host of other prices–such as, interest rates, remuneration rates for rural teachers, health personnel, and extension workers. In this view the distorted structure of incentives as evidenced by the price system enables the urban sector to lay first claim to resources whose scarcity is artificially created and maintained. Do away with these distortions, it is claimed, and we can create a viable rural economy without having to trouble much with institution-building, private institutions in many cases being able to enter to take advantage of new profit opportunities or to avoid losses that would otherwise be sustained. Thus it may be possible to argue that raising bank interest rates would lead commercial banks to attempt to release available excess funds to the capital-scarce agricultural sector.

I will not pause here to argue the merits or demerits of this line of argument. Clearly in its most extreme form presented above, it is false. There is however, much truth in it, particularly as applied to Thailand. Whatever the case may be, it cannot be denied that if attempts were made to apply the corrective suggested by the above argument, there would be a massive transfer of resources from the urban *back* to the rural sector.

In this view, the resources are there to be tapped in the urban sector, if only it can be persuaded to part with them. There is no need for foreign aid of any kind because what needs correction is the distorted price system. An absolute shortage is ruled out by assumption.

Distortions in the domestic price system are not the only factor to be taken into account. In fact, changes in the international price structure are much more important. Discussions concerning development and foreign aid from the late 1950s into the 1960s typically omitted this factor, perhaps because they took place in the context of relatively stable world prices. Even now, discussions of foreign aid and development problems frequently assume fixed prices, explicitly or implicitly. And in the atypical instances in which this assumption is dropped, the anticipated adjustments in prices are assumed to be small. Similarly, in few of the two-sector models in which the terms of trade between rural and urban sectors are mentioned are the full implications drawn. As a result, much of the modeling for developing countries ends up by projecting various kinds of gaps and deficits. These gaps and deficits, it is then alleged, can only be bridged by drawing on foreign resources, as exchange rate adjustments are regarded generally as an old-fashioned remedy, incapable of dealing with basic structural problems.

There has been some reaction not only against such cavalier dismissals of exchange rate adjustments, but also against underemphasis of the problems to which such adjustments are a response. The set of OECD studies summarized in Little, Scitovsky and Scott is a notable example,[6] clearly pointing out the extent of the distortions in most underdeveloped countries that arise from changes in the international price structure. What really gave point to such studies was the commodity boom of 1973 and 1974. Suddenly, all the old discussions of foreign aid became irrelevant.

Take the case of Thailand. The peak year for foreign inflow of resources during the 1960s seems to have been 1968, when 1407.1 million baht was received as grants and 758.4 billion baht of *gross* borrowing by the Central Bank took place, making a total of 2165.5 million baht.[7] Compared with the approximately 8,000 million baht that the new oil prices alone are expected to add to the import bill, or with the somewhat larger addition to our export earnings attributable solely to the increase in the prices of our food exports, the small magnitude of the sums involved in "foreign aid" becomes evident.

The same applies to the impact of price changes on rural-urban income differentials. The commodity boom has definitely had a favorable impact on agricultural incomes in Thailand, notwithstanding the rise in fertilizer prices. The exact magnitude of this increase in income during the past two years is not clear, but one should consider the following facts.

a. Rice prices have approximately trebled: Maize prices have risen to 2½ times their previous levels.
b. Fertilizer costs have quintupled but amount to only about 10 percent of the present selling prices of the commodities. Only a minority of Thai farmers use fertilizers.
c. Fuel costs for most farm machines form an even smaller proportion of the total selling price.

Fertilizers and fuel are the only two purchased inputs of which the prices have risen substantially. Most other inputs and the farmer's own living expenses have gone up far less.

It is thus safe to conclude that agricultural incomes in Thailand have increased in the past two years. One might even hazard the guess that the gains to the farmers as a result of the price changes of 1973 and 1974 probably exceed the gains accruing to them as a result of all past government efforts to increase their incomes.

In the context of the violently changing prices of the 1970s, what foreign aid can achieve directly, particularly for agriculture, is essentially very little. This must be borne in mind in assessing the role of foreign aid and in recognizing the pointlessness of projections into the 1980s which relate foreign aid and rural development while implicitly assuming a predictable fixed-price world that was left behind in the 1960s.

When we examine the impact of the commodity boom of 1973-1974 on rural-urban differences, even though very little hard data exist, it is highly probable that this impact has been generally favorable to the rural sector. Within the urban sector, raising the minimum wage rates during the same two years has not led to much unemployment—primarily because with better agricultural incomes, the rural inflow into Bangkok has probably slowed down. The new minimum wage rates are thus tenable rates. With higher wages and little unemployment, distribution of urban incomes is thus probably improved.

The above leap into speculation about the unknown effects of the commodity boom can yield only tentative results. What is definite, however, is the importance, in terms of order of magnitude, of the kind of price changes that took place in the past two years, which makes all the discussions of foreign aid that depend for their conclusions largely on the magnitude of such aid even more academic than before.

I have been very negative about the role of foreign aid in my presentation because I have tended to look at the matter from a narrowly economic perspective. I conclude that apart from the benefits to be gained from further technological progress, which to a certain extent can be stimulated with foreign assistance, the bulk of serious rural development has to be at the expense of the urban sector, and foreign aid has little role to play in such circumstances.

Let me suggest one final possibility, i.e., foreign aid as social anaesthesia. If the urban sector is to be made to part with so much of its resources, it may need to be bribed to do so. Foreign aid could play a role in such bribery. But having suggested the possibility, let me hastily drop the matter, as political science is not my specialty.

**Notes**

1. W.W. Rostow, *The Stages of Economic Growth: A Non-Communist Manifesto*, (Cambridge: Cambridge University Press, 1961).

2. R.I. McKinnon, "Foreign Exchange Constraints in Economic Development and Efficient Aid Allocation," *Economic Journal*, June, 1964.

3. H. Chenery and A. Strout, "Foreign Assistance and Economic Development," *American Economic Review*, September, 1966.

4. "Practical men, who believe themselves to be quite exempt from any intellectual influences, are usually the slaves of some defunct economist." J.M. Keynes, *The General Theory of Employment Interest and Money* (New York: Harcourt Brace Jovanovitch, Inc., 1936), p. 383.

5. Y. Hayami and V. Ruttan, *Agricultural Development* (Baltimore: The Johns Hopkins University Press, 1972).

6. I.M.D. Little, T. Scitovsky, and M. Scott, *Industry and Trade in Some Developing Countries: A Comparative Study* (Oxford: Oxford University Press, 1970).

7. Bank of Thailand figures.

## Discussion: The Ammar Paper

In presenting his paper to the Seminar, Ammar reemphasized his point that foreign aid has only a minor role to play when the objective of development becomes rearrangement of the economic and social structure of a nation—a point that stimulated a great deal of discussion. On more specific issues, he noted that a major problem in the future will be land availability. As population grows, farm sizes will get smaller, and there is little that land reform alone can do to deal with this problem. Small farmers will require personalized assistance rather than the construction of more roads and dams, and extension services will have to be very diverse and adapted to a variety of local needs. The need for such personalized services can be met only through effective delivery systems, including extension workers who are sensitive to individual problems and the unique characteristics of each local situation. Turning to the final point of his paper, that domestic price distortions are a major barrier to effective rural development, Ammar added that the additional fact must be recognized that the recent enormous rise in world prices has dwarfed foreign aid in the sheer quantitative magnitude of its impact both on rice export receipts and the costs of import-related agricultural inputs—another point that had a telling effect upon the participants. Future world price changes may make current estimates of the effects of aid quite misleading.

Discussion following this paper was wide-ranging. Several participants pursued Ammar's contention that new types of services and delivery systems—institutional innovations, in his words—were required to raise the overall income level in the rural sector and simultaneously reduce, or at least not increase, income inequalities in that sector. It was noted that priorities in extension work must be set, and that perhaps, to achieve social goals, extension workers in fields such as nursing and education would be needed as much if not more than those versed in technical and economic aspects of agriculture and farm management. It was added that unless the rate of population growth can be reduced, nothing else really matters. One participant stated that he had found extension workers to be dedicated people, but not supplied with adequate funds or equipment to do their jobs, not well educated, and not provided with incentives to do their jobs properly. Ammar responded by saying that he believed the basic problem was the incentive structure: Extension workers were not selected by the local people, not responsible to them, nor evaluated by them. In Ammar's opinion, if people in the area served by an extension worker, rather than a ministry in Bangkok, were in a position to influence the extension worker's salary and promotion, the situation would be greatly improved. In the opinion of a number of participants, the only practical way to improve delivery services to the rural areas is through the intermediate step of developing and improving the facilities in urban areas outside of Bangkok. For example, far better hospital facilities in towns such as

Ayudhaya and Khon Kaen would be a precondition for stimulating a flow of doctors and nurses out of Bangkok and into rural areas surrounding these towns. One participant maintained that there was certainly no way evident to him by which traditional foreign aid could assist in Ammar's "bottom up" transfer of resources, and the role of such aid in providing effective delivery systems would be quite limited. He suggested that expansion of foreign trade could stimulate development of domestic delivery systems within the private sector, as well as avoiding the violation of concepts of self-reliance and political integrity being discussed at the Seminar. He asked if policies of foreign nations designed to promote trade with Thailand should be included in a more meaningful definition of "aid." Ammar's point that population increase will lead to more small-sized farms prompted the observation that successful small-scale farming requires widespread access to capital and credit and fairly high levels of education and know-how on the part of farmers. These, it was suggested, are the crucial elements to be handled by an effective delivery system.

The second of the two major problems identified by Ammar, distortions in the price system, also became a subject of varied discussion. Reservations were expressed about the ability of the price system to function effectively when some groups are weak and possess no market power. Accordingly, it was suggested that only after groups, such as farmers, workers and slum-dwellers, have come together and organized themselves into collective bargaining, buying, or selling organizations will it make sense to rely on the price system. Ammar disagreed, arguing that price distortions created by the government itself, such as the rice premium, were far more harmful to farmers than any exploitation by traditional villains such as middlemen and money lenders. Simply getting the government out of the rice and sugar trades, for example, would be of far more benefit than anything that could conceivably be done to improve the structures of intermediate markets. In following up on the point made about encouragement of trade being in fact a form of aid, criticism was leveled at the conduct of foreign nations and firms. Donor countries, it was contended, could and should begin liberalizing their trade systems. Foreign firms play major roles in the marketing of the principal Thai agricultural products and, in the opinion of at least one participant, engage in many restrictive and anticompetitive devices in Thailand that are prohibited by the laws of their home countries. There was some rather inconclusive discussion about the need for antitrust or restrictive practices legislation in Thailand, it being concluded that Thais should be studying foreign laws dealing with monopolies and trade restrictions but that the antitrust laws of, say, Japan or the U.S. could not be simply imported to Thailand as they stand.

It was suggested that rising import prices might heighten the need for aid. Ammar agreed, responding that the point he wished to make about the impact of rising world prices was that no reasonably conceivable level of aid could close the gap being caused by worldwide inflation.

Puey pursued the question of self-reliance, commenting that he disagreed with the point that had been made earlier that grants and long-term, low-interest loans are interchangeable. Self-reliance required an end to grants sooner or later, but since Thailand had helped to create such international credit institutions as the IBRD and the Asian Development Bank (ADB), the country should have no reluctance about continuing to make use of their loan services. Discussion of the transfer of technology led to the observation that it is far more difficult to transfer useful knowledge from one culture to another in the social sciences than in the physical or medical sciences. It is important for Thailand to become self-reliant in this respect, although no nation ought ever try to become self-sufficient in the sense of isolating itself from the international exchange of ideas. Thus, Puey contended, the fact that well-trained and educated Thais in responsible positions still want to have foreign advisors assigned to them is not a healthy sign. Another participant noted that application of Puey's concept of self-reliance to rural areas called for a type of social and economic development in the countryside to which foreign aid could contribute very little. Indeed, he continued, there was a danger that aid-supported projects might retard this development, as a sort of "social service" activity. He suggested, however, that foreign aid could be of use in providing the resources for specific integrated rural development projects, in which relatively small areas were subjected to concentrated interrelated aid projects as demonstrations of what might be done throughout the nation by its own effort.

The appropriate definition of "aid" was discussed further. Should it include foreign private investment as analyzed in the paper by Sura and Twatchai as well as the trade policies of foreign nations? Ammar suggested defining aid as "a transfer of resources from rich countries to poor ones, made by decisions of public bodies." Public bodies, he noted, would include multilateral agencies as well as nations. Under this definition, liberal trade policies would certainly be included. So would such actions as that of the U.S. Congress in voting to pay higher than world prices for sugar from certain nations. On the other hand, Ammar concluded, to the extent that prices paid or received by Thailand are affected adversely by the decisions of foreign nations or their instruments, a moral claim to aid arises.

# Foreign Aid and the Choice of Technique in Road Construction in Thailand

William A. McCleary

## Introduction

In recent years many developing countries have discovered that even fairly rapid economic growth need not create sufficient employment opportunities for the growing labor force and that growth has often been accompanied by rising rates of unemployment, particularly in urban areas. While the phenomenon of large open unemployment in urban centers and disguised unemployment in rural areas does not appear to be as severe in Thailand as in other Asian countries–notably India, Pakistan, Ceylon, Bangladesh, and the Philippines–there is evidence of a present and growing problem. The phenomenon of seasonality in agricultural employment, dominated by seasonality in rice farming, is already well documented for Thailand. Comparing total hours worked with total hours available for work, it is evident that in the northern and northeastern regions, the two poorest regions in the country, there is some unemployment throughout the year but that in the dry season the rate passes the 50 percent mark; for other regions the same pattern exists but is not so pronounced. Moreover, while there is some evidence that the timing of seasonal downswings in agricultural employment is matched by seasonal upswings in services and manufacturing employment, it seems clear that substantial numbers either become unemployed or drop out of the labor force.[1] In addition, a recent study has shown that as a result of rapid population growth in Thailand over the past two decades, the rate of growth of the labor force is expected to expand from the late 1960s rate of about 2.5 percent per annum to about 3 percent per annum over the 1970 to 1985 period.[2] This study and two further studies,[3] on the basis of admittedly crude assumptions about labor force participation rates, growth rates of nonagricultural output, and sector output-employment ratios, predict greater unemployment and a growing necessity to absorb labor productively in the rural areas.

In the face of such evidence, it would appear prudent both to examine relative-factor prices in the Thai economy to determine whether market prices

The research on which this short paper was based was financed by a grant from the International Labor Office to the Faculty of Economics, Thammasat University (Bangkok) for a "Research Project on Labor Intensive Techniques in Road Construction in Thailand." The author is grateful to the four engineers provided by ILO who supplied the engineering inputs for this study: Alan Heap, Colin Relf, Hans Boisen, and most particularly, Bertil Nilssen. They of course share any credit–but not any blame–due the author for the study which follows.

have an antilabor-intensive bias and to explore the possibilities for providing more productive employment opportunities in the rural sector. It was in this spirit that, a little over a year ago, the International Labor Office sponsored a group of engineers and Thammasat University economists to explore the possibilities of labor-intensive road construction in Thailand. (Similar studies were sponsored in Iran, Nepal, and the Philippines.) The purpose of these studies was to establish capital-intensive and labor-intensive techniques for the various activities in road construction, compare the costs of the alternative techniques measured at market prices, determine the extent to which market prices for factor inputs depart from social costs, and compare the social costs of alternative techniques.[a] The paper begins by presenting a simple methodology for analyzing these questions given the limited data available on the nature of the production function in road construction. It then summarizes the findings for Thailand in terms of the costs of alternative techniques at market prices and social costs. Moreover, it is often hypothesized that foreign aid influences the choice of production technique. By lowering the cost of imported inputs relative to labor (and other domestically produced inputs), aid is said to create incentives for more capital-intensive methods of production than would have been chosen in the absence of aid. In the final section of this paper, we examine the nature of aid terms that creates this bias and provide some crude estimates of the size of the bias given various alternative assumptions about aid terms.

## The Problem Outlined

It is possible to obtain a clear view of the problem under study using the isoquant-isocost analysis familar to economists. The production function, which is the relationship between physical inputs of labor and capital (and other factors) and physical outputs of product, may be represented in two dimensions (for a two-factor case) by a family of isoquants, each of which shows all of the combinations of capital and labor inputs that can be used to produce a given level of output [see Figure 5-1(a)]. One such curve has been labeled 100 to reflect the fact that it shows those combinations of factor inputs that can be used to produce 100 units of output; curves representing greater outputs would lie everywhere above and to the right of this curve, and conversely. To determine which is the optimum (or least-cost) combination of factors for producing 100 units of output, it is necessary to know the costs of labor inputs *relative* to the cost of equipment inputs. Isocost curves show all of the combinations of (physical inputs of) labor and capital that can be purchased for the same total cost [see line *AB* in Figure 5-1(a)]; the slope of an isocost is the ratio of the

[a]The results of this study are reported in W.A. McCleary, *A Social Cost Analysis of Alternative Techniques of Road Construction in Thailand* (Geneva: International Labor Office; forthcoming, title tentative).

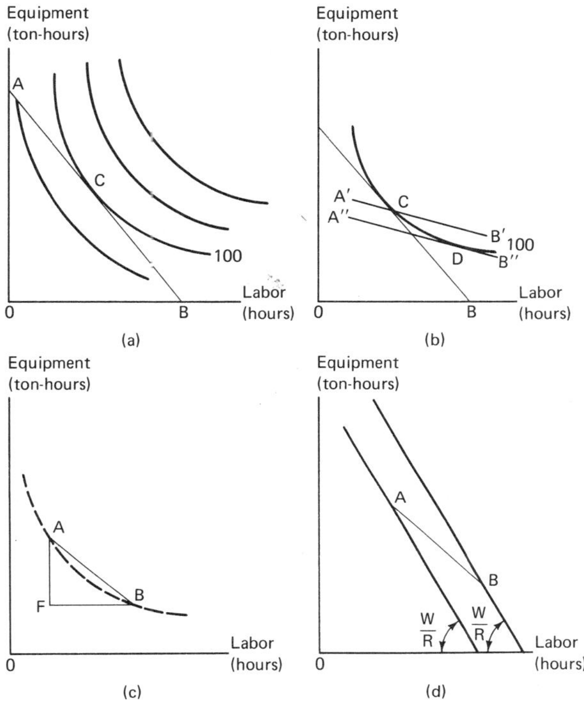


**Figure 5-1.** Isoquant–Isocost Analysis

wage rate to the rental rate on capital equipment (the rental rate being that charge which, if attributed to every working hour over the machine's lifetime, would have the same present value as the costs of owning and operating the machine over that period). Isocosts representing higher money costs than *AB* would lie above and to the right, and conversely. The least-cost output occurs where the slopes of the isoquant and isocost are equal [point *C* in Figure 5-1(a)]; it can be seen readily that the isocost curves at any other point on the given isoquant must be higher than *AB*). Note that it is only relative-factor prices that matter; if wages and rentals were both to increase by *x* percent, the least-cost combination of factor inputs for producing 100 units of output would still be at *C*. (Of course, the total cost of producing that output would be *x* percent higher.) On the other hand, if wages fall relative to rentals, *C* will no longer be the least-cost combination. The isocost at *C* reflecting the new relative factor prices will have a less steep slope than that of the isoquant at *C* [see *A'B'* in Figure 5-1(b)]. Clearly the least-cost combination of factors lies at a point further down on the isoquant where the slope of the isoquant will be equal to the (less steep) slope of the isocost lines [see point *D* in Figure 5-1(b)]. The result, involving larger labor inputs and smaller capital inputs, is in accord with common sense: Cheapening labor inputs relative to capital inputs results in the substitution of labor for capital. The result would have been the same had rental rates risen with wage rates constant in such a way as to bring about the same wage to rental ratio [as reflected in the slopes of $A'B'$ and $A''B''$ in Figure 5-1(b)]. This simple example illustrates a basic principle that is key to understanding the empirical study that follows: The greater the costs of labor inputs relative to the costs of capital inputs, the futher to the left on the isoquant the least-cost combination will lie (i.e., the more capital-intensive production will be) and conversely.

It is easy to cast the problem of the choice of technique in road construction in Thailand in a framework similar to that used above. It is possible to analyze the construction of a typical feeder road in terms of about 19 production activities (e.g., clearing, excavation of common soil, hauling soil and rock various distances, etc.). Each of these activities can be thought of in terms of a specified physical output (e.g., hectares to be cleared, cubic meters of earth to be excavated and hauled, etc.) to be carried out by specified quantities of labor and capital inputs. For a typical feeder road 10 kilometers in length, a team of ILO engineers has specified the quantities of each activity necessary to complete the road. On the basis of interviews with Highway Department officials, local and foreign contractors, and highway consulting firms, and reference to published productivity figures, this engineering team has established productivity figures for equipment and labor in various phases of road construction and, for most activities, has established two (sometimes three) alternative combinations of capital and labor necessary to complete the specified output for each activity: one capital-intensive method, one labor-intensive method, and sometimes a third intermediate method. Thus in graphical terms for any activity there are two points ($A$ and $B$) thought on the basis of existing evidence to lie on the same isoquant. The remainder of the isoquant remains unknown [hence, in Figure 5-1(c) the isoquant is drawn as a dotted line indicating that its exact shape is unknown]. Obviously a large number of isoquants of different shapes can pass through points $A$ and $B$.

However, it is still possible to measure the slope of line $AB$; in terms of Figure 5-1(c), it is $AF/FB$. Designating the quantities of capital and labor inputs at $A$ as $K_1, L_1$ and at $B$ as $K_2, L_2$

$$\frac{AF}{FB} = \frac{K_1 - K_2}{L_1 - L_2}.$$

We will call this slope "the Average Rate of Technical Substitution between $A$ and $B$" ($ARTS_{ab}$—this terminology distinguishes this slope from the marginal rate of technical substitution which is the slope of an isoquant at a point). Given the wage rate and the rental rate, we can then say that if $W/R > ARTS_{ab}$, point

$A$ will be preferred to point $B$ in the sense that the costs of performing that activity will be lower at $A$ than $B$, and conversely. Graphically, it is easy to see why: if $W/R > \text{ARTS}_{ab}$, point $A$ clearly lies on a lower isocost curve than point $B$ [see Figure 5-1(d)]. Obviously then, if $W/R = \text{ARTS}_{ab}$, both $A$ and $B$ will be equally costly. Note, however, that although this procedure allows us to establish whether $A$ is preferred to $B$, it does not allow us to determine whether the preferred point is, in fact, an optimum; it can only be said that the preferred point is an optimum if we know that the slope of the isoquant at the preferred point is equal to $W/R$, but we have no way of knowing this without more complete information about the slope of the relevant isoquant (e.g., if $W/R = \text{ARTS}_{ab}$, the optimum would lie somewhere between $A$ and $B$).[b]

Given the above framework, it is necessary to be able to measure the relative costs of equipment and unskilled labor inputs both at market prices and social costs. Market price data for all input items into road construction were gathered on the basis of published information and interviews with contractors and equipment and materials suppliers in Thailand. On this basis it was possible to derive a cost-of-construction-at-market-prices figure for every activity, for both capital-intensive and labor-intensive (and, where applicable, intermediate) techniques. A problem arises from the fact that, whereas the framework uses two factor inputs—equipment and unskilled labor—in reality, there are five broad classes of inputs into road construction: equipment, materials (cement, dynamite, etc.), implements (hand tools such as axes, saws, etc.), skilled labor, and unskilled labor. This problem is handled easily because all the other inputs may either be treated as complementary to the use of equipment and unskilled labor inputs or be eliminated because they do not affect the question of substituting unskilled labor for capital. Thus the use of equipment requires skilled labor in the form of operators and foreman supervisors; the use of unskilled labor requires implements and foreman supervision. Inputs of materials are exactly the same for both capital-intensive and labor-intensive techniques and hence can be eliminated from the relative-cost ratios. In this fashion all the costs of other factor inputs can be assigned to either equipment or unskilled labor costs. This

[b]The reader who is familiar with road construction will realize that a large number of problems have not been dealt with in the above discussion. These are treated more completely in McCleary, op. cit., but here we can at least briefly outline their nature. The problems stem from the prevailing lack of knowledge about the nature of the production function in all activities of road construction. Some of the more important open questions are: (1) Is the nature of the isoquant between $A$ and $B$ known at least for some points? It appears that most countries use either very capital-intensive or very labor-intensive techniques of construction, and hence it is very difficult for engineers to specify the types and amounts of equipment and labor to be used in an intermediate method that would produce the same level of output. (2) What is the nature of returns to scale in each activity? Does the ability to substitute labor for capital depend on the level of output? (Crudely, would the slope of the ARTS for any activity vary much as the level of output varied?) (3) The productivity of labor and capital in the various phases of road construction is known to be affected by changes in environmental conditions—e.g., weather, soil conditions, terrain, etc. Do changes in these environmental conditions seriously affect the ability to substitute labor for capital?

fact, of course, applies regardless of whether costs are measured in market price or social cost terms. The cost of an hour of equipment input now becomes the hourly rental plus the hourly operator and supervision costs; similarly, the cost of an hour of unskilled labor input becomes the hourly wage of an unskilled worker plus an hourly implements and supervision charge. To designate the fact that we have altered our definitions of relative factor costs, we will use the symbols $\hat{W}^m/\hat{R}^m$ when costs are at market prices and $\hat{W}^{AC}/\hat{R}^{AC}$ when at social costs. It is assumed that funds to pay construction costs are acquired by government through increased taxation; the source of funds does not affect costs when the latter are measured at market prices but does affect them when they are measured in social-cost terms.

In a paper of this length, it is impossible to explain adequately the conversion of costs at market prices into social-cost terms. Therefore, only a brief explanation will be given. The procedures used followed closely those in the UNIDO *Guidelines for Project Evaluation* (written by A.K. Sen, Stephen Marglin, and Partha Das Gupta).[4] Briefly, three major adjustments were made:

1. All costs were measured in terms of the aggregate consumption sacrificed by the Thai economy. Thus, when resources are obtained for the project at the expense of current consumption, Thailand's sacrifice is correctly measured at market prices (sometimes, where necessary, with adjustments for taxes or foreign exchange embodied in market prices). However, when resources are obtained at the expense of current investment, the sacrifice is the present value of future consumption which such investment would have made possible. If aggregate investment (savings) were optimal, the present value of future consumption would be equal to the value of current investment measured at market prices. If, as seems to be the case, Thai planners and policymakers feel that a higher savings rate would be desirable (i.e., that aggregate savings are suboptimal), this value judgment is expressed in the fact that the marginal rate of return on aggregate investment is greater than the social rate of discount. In this event, the aggregate consumption cost or shadow price of investment is greater than one. If so, the sources by which projects are financed will definitely affect the costs of projects; the more project finance reduces current investment rather than current consumption, the greater the aggregate consumption cost of the project will be. Thus all project costs were converted to aggregate consumption cost terms on the assumption that project costs were financed out of additional taxation; aggregate consumption costs are thus dependent on the marginal propensities of taxpayers to consume and save.

2. A second adjustment was made for the foreign exchange costs of the project. In a situation where trade is subject to various tariffs, taxes, and subsidies, the official exchange rate no longer correctly measures the value of an additional unit of foreign exchange to the economy. To take an example, a dollar's worth of foreign exchange can be used to buy goods worth a dollar (CIF) or approximately 20 baht for the goods that a dollar's worth of foreign

exchange makes available. At the margin, one dollar is worth 30 baht in terms of the value that consumers place on the imports which that dollar makes possible. Similarly, were exports subject to a 25 percent tax, earning an additional dollar's worth of foreign exchange through exports requires the sacrifice of goods which consumers would value at 15 baht at the margin. Generalizing from these simple examples, the shadow price for foreign exchange becomes the official exchange rate times one plus the sum of the weighted average tariff (plus other taxes) on imports and the weighted average tax (or subsidy) on exports. Given the present system of trade taxation in Thailand (plus some adjustments made to account for the present abnormal rice taxes and export quotas), we estimated the shadow price of foreign exchange in Thailand to be about 15 percent above the official rate. Thus the import content of all project inputs (valued CIF) was reevaluated at the shadow price of foreign exchange; at the same time the tariff and tax component of the domestic market price for each of these goods was removed as such transfer payments involve no real costs to the economy (except that the transfer of income from taypayers to the government involved an aggregate consumption cost as taxpayers were estimated to have a higher marginal propensity to save than the government; the adjustments to account for this fact were extremely small).

3. The last adjustment involved the wage of unskilled workers on the project, which was estimated to be an inaccurate measure of the real costs to society. This adjustment involved two steps, the first to reflect the fact that the project wage overstates the real cost to society of employing an additional unskilled worker (this overstatement appears to be very small in the Thai case, however), and the second to reflect the fact that a project wage in excess of real costs is essentially a redistribution of income from taxpayers to workers which may impose an additional cost on society if the marginal propensity of taxpayers to save exceeds that of unskilled workers. An interesting byproduct of the latter adjustment is our finding that, contrary to what is usually assumed in the literature on development economics and project evaluation in developing countries, the marginal propensity to save out of rural household income (per capita) in Thailand is not zero or negligible; hence, given the regressive nature of the Thai tax system, the redistribution that accompanies the employment of additional unskilled rural workers on a project will not impose a cost on society in the form of reduced aggregate savings. On the basis of the above adjustments, we find that the aggregate consumption cost of an unskilled worker is about 90 percent of the hourly wage when a 15 percent social discount rate is used and about 15 percent above the market wage when a 10 percent discount rate is employed.

If, by now, some readers are thoroughly puzzled by the social cost adjustments we have made, they have our sympathy, for explanation has of necessity been rather terse. Their confusion, however, need not deter their understanding the remaining two sections of this paper if they follow this guideline. For each activity, there is a measured ARTS and three ratios $\hat{W}^m/\hat{R}^m$, $\hat{W}^{AC}_{10}/\hat{R}^{AC}_{10}$, and $\hat{W}^{AC}_{15}/\hat{R}^{AC}_{15}$, the latter two being 15 percent and 10 percent social discount rates, respectively. For every activity, the answers to two questions are sought. (1) Given the ratio of factor costs at market prices and the ARTS, are labor-intensive (or intermediate) methods cheaper than capital-intensive methods? (2) If a switch from relative factor costs at market prices to those at social cost (or aggregate consumption cost) is made, in what way, if at all, will the choice of (the least-cost) technique be affected?

## The Efficiency of Alternative Techniques of Road Construction at Market Prices and Social Costs

In Table 5-1, the results of our analysis are presented for 12 out of the 19 identified tasks (or activities) involved in feeder road construction.[c] The remaining 7 tasks have been omitted from this paper because they involved either cases where no substitution between labor and capital was possible or cases where the amount of additional employment generated by a switch from the capital-intensive to the labor-intensive technique was relatively minor. For each task there is an ARTS (column 1), a ratio of factor costs at market prices (column 2), two ratios for relative-factor costs at social costs for 15 percent, and 10 percent social discount rates (columns 3 and 4). The conclusions that may be derived from these results are summarized as follows.

1. Using relative-factor costs measured at market prices, in not one out of the twelve activities will the labor-intensive method be favored over the capital-intensive method; the relative-factor cost ratios in column 2 are always higher than the ARTS in column 1. The total costs of construction for labor-intensive methods in the various tasks range from 5 percent to 84 percent higher than those for capital-intensive methods (data supporting this statement is not shown). Labor-intensive methods are less than 25 percent more expensive in activities 1, 8, 10, 11, and 12 but are more than 50 percent more expensive in activities 4, 5, 6, 7, and 9.[5]

2. When alternative techniques are costed at aggregate consumption costs, the cost of the labor-intensive technique is equal to that of the capital-intensive technique only for task 1 but is less than 10 percent more expensive in tasks 2, 8, 10, 11, and 12 when a 15 percent social discount rate is used. At a 10 percent

[c] In this paper we will use the terms "task" and "activity" as if they were interchangeable. In an effort to standardize terminology on road construction studies, the ILO and IBRD have agreed to use "task" to identify high levels of aggregation in work performed and "activity" for the disaggregation of "tasks" into the component work items–e.g., the "task" of "Excavation of Common Soil, 50 Meter Haul" would be composed of the following "activities": excavation, loading, hauling, unloading, and spreading. Since in this paper we will always be talking about results for a high level of aggregation, there is no danger of confusion between the two terms.

**Table 5-1**
**The Average Rate of Technical Substitution Between Labor and Capital, the Ratios of Labor Costs to Equipment Costs at Market Prices, and Aggregate Consumption Costs**

| | ARTS (1) | $\hat{W}^m/\hat{R}^m$ (2) | $\hat{W}^{AC}/\hat{R}^{AC}$ 15% Social Discount Rate (3) | $\hat{W}^{AC}/\hat{R}^{AC}$ 10% Social Discount Rate (4) |
|---|---|---|---|---|
| 1. Clearing | –.149 | –.169 | –.150 | –.155 |
| 2. Grubbing | –.093 | –.120 | –.100 | –.103 |
| 3. Excavation Common Soil: Haul 50 m | –.087 | –.128 | –.107 | –.111 |
| 4. Excavation Common Soil: Haul 700 m | –.106 | –.165 | –.147 | –.152 |
| 5. Excavation Soft Rock: Haul 25 m | –.069 | –.128 | –.106 | –.110 |
| 6. Excavation Soft Rock: Haul 700 m | –.089 | –.135 | –.117 | –.120 |
| 7. Excavation Solid Rock: Drilling and Blasting | –.022 | –.036 | –.030 | –.034 |
| 8. Excavation Solid Rock: Haul 25 m | –.114 | –.148 | –.119 | –.124 |
| 9. Excavation Solid Rock: Haul 200 m | –.097 | –.151 | –.137 | –.139 |
| 10. Embankment | –.135 | –.200 | –.165 | –.175 |
| 11. Embankment: Selected Material | –.172 | –.200 | –.199 | –.199 |
| 12. Gravel Base and Shoulders | –.139 | –.240 | –.199 | –.199 |

social discount rate, labor-intensive methods are more expensive than capital-intensive methods in all tasks, but the costs exceed those of capital-intensive methods by from 3.6 percent to 12.8 percent in tasks 1, 2, 8, 10, 11, and 12.[6]

3. Whether a 15 percent or a 10 percent social discount rate is used, accounting in terms of aggregate consumption costs raises the costs of equipment inputs relative to labor inputs (i.e., the relative-factor cost ratios in columns 3 and 4 are always lower than the corresponding ratios in column 2).

4. The reduction in the relative-factor cost ratios from what they were at market prices is smaller for a 10 percent social discount rate than for a 15 percent rate (i.e., the factor cost ratios in column 4 are always higher than those in column 3). This finding is in accordance with economic theory: A lower discount rate means a smaller penalty on the value of future consumption relative to present consumption and hence favors more investment, projects of longer duration, and more capital-intensity (or less labor-intensity) in production techniques.

5. Perhaps most importantly, the fact that accounting in terms of aggregate consumption costs lowers the cost of labor inputs relative to those for equipment inputs strongly suggests that in all activities the adoption of some technique less capital-intensive than the one favored at market prices would result in a gain for society in the form of reduced aggregate consumption costs. However, how much more labor-intensity (less capital-intensity) would be desirable cannot be determined in the absence of further knowledge about the nature of the shape of the isoquant between our two identified techniques.

In sum, the above findings show that at market prices, capital-intensive methods clearly involved lower costs than labor-intensive or intermediate methods. Thus the highly capital-intensive methods one finds in road construction, whether by government agencies or by private contractors, appears at least in part to be a rational attempt at cost-minimization given the structure of incentives faced at market prices. If costs are measured in social terms instead, a switch from the capital-intensive to the labor-intensive alternative identified by our team of engineers would not appear justified in most instances. However, our results indicate clearly that less capital-intensity than is justified at market prices would be desirable for Thailand–i.e., it would reduce the aggregate consumption costs of road construction resulting in a net gain for society as a whole. This justification rests on a pure efficiency criterion; it does not take account of the fact that the greater employment generated might have desirable effects from the point of view of income distribution, political stability, etc. However, these findings raise a dilemma: Not much appears to be known about the nature of the production function in various activities between the alternatives of extreme capital-intensity and extreme labor-intensity; the desirability of a move toward greater labor-intensity than presently exists appears to rest on the ability of engineers to design efficient intermediate techniques.

## Foreign Aid and the Choice of Technique

It is often said that the use of foreign aid to finance projects affects the choice of technique used in the construction of such projects. Where aid is tied to imports and to particular projects, it reduces the cost of imported capital goods (as well as any other imported goods covered by aid) relative to the cost of labor (and domestically produced goods), thus inducing countries to use more capital-intensive techniques than they would have used had the cost of the project been financed from local resources. In the previous section of this paper, we showed that the relative costs of alternative techniques of road construction tend to favor the capital-intensive over the labor-intensive technique in the vast majority of cases both when costs are measured at market prices and at aggregate consumption cost given that construction costs would be covered by local taxation. These calculations allowed for the use of imported equipment, the foreign exchange, cost of which was valued at the official exchange rate when market prices were used to measure costs, and at the shadow price of foreign exchange when aggregate consumption costs were being estimated. When the import content of a project will be covered by a loan or grant, it is necessary to recalculate the aggregate consumption costs to the economy, given the fact that foreign exchange content is loan- or grant-financed and that local content is financed by taxation. In this fashion it will be possible to determine the effects of aid on equipment rentals and on the ratio of the cost of labor inputs to equipment inputs, and hence to calculate the size of the ultimate bias toward capital-intensity.

The opportunity cost to the economy of a loan tied to a project is the present value of the repayments of interest and principal occasioned by the loan; the loan creates no present costs since the economy gives up no real resources in the present, but the repayment of principal and interest in the future imposes a real cost on the economy that is clearly the result of the project. The opportunity cost of a grant is obviously zero since the economy gives up no resources either in the present or the future. The size of the opportunity cost imposed by a loan depends on the interest rate charged on the unrepaid portion of principal, the length of the grace period (during which time no repayments of principal are required but payments of interest may be required), the length of the repayment period, and the pattern of repayments of principal over the repayment period. The loan terms that we have taken as an example are typical of the terms of a World Bank loan to Thailand: (1) 7 1/4 percent interest per annum is charged on the withdrawn but as yet unrepaid portion of principal;[d] (2) the grace period is five years; and (3) the repayment extends over a twenty-year period following the end of the grace period with a pattern of repayment of principal such that the sum of principal and interest payments are approximately equal for each of the twenty years. Given this information, it is possible to calculate a present value for this stream of payments. At a 15 percent social discount rate, it

[d]The actual terms are somewhat more complicated than this. When the Bank makes a commitment for a loan, the recipient draws upon the loan proceeds as cost items covered by the loan come due for payment. The Bank charges ¾ percent service charge on the committed but as yet not withdrawn part of the loan and a 7¼ percent interest charge on the withdrawn but as yet unrepaid portion. In our calculations we have taken account of both charges by using a predicted schedule of loan withdrawals.

represents a cost to Thailand of 65.3 baht for every 100 baht of loan received; for a 10 percent social discount rate, the cost is 87.9 baht per 100 baht of loan received. In the lingo of aid economics, given the loan terms and the social discount rate, the former has a "grant element" of 34.7 percent, the latter 12.1 percent.[e] That is, in the former case Thailand would be as well off if it received a 34.7 baht grant as it would have been with a 100 baht loan on these terms; in the latter case a 12.1 baht grant or a 100 baht loan on the stated terms would be equally valuable.

Given the fact that rental rates can be broken down into foreign exchange, local, and tax-tariff costs, it is possible to recalculate the aggregate consumption cost rental rates using the foregoing information. Before doing so, two further complications necessitated by the realities of the Thai case must be noted.

1. Since payments of loan principal and interest will take place in foreign exchange and since we have said that there is a differential between the official exchange rate and the shadow exchange rate, it is necessary to ask how this differential will behave over the next 25 years to calculate the present value of loan payments—that is, each year's payments should be valued at the shadow price of foreign exchange for that year. Obviously, this is a formidable problem. Since we are in no position to attempt such a forecast, the accuracy of which would be open to extreme doubt in any case, it will be assumed that the shadow price of foreign exchange remains constant over the period—i.e., there will continue to be a premium of 15 percent on foreign exchange for the next 25 years. If one assumes that, as development proceeds, Thailand will reduce tariffs and export duties (since it seems plausible that a country would move toward "freer trade" as development progresses), the premium should be lowered over time. This of course would lower the present value of loan payments and raise the "grant element" in aid; hence our assumption of constancy in the shadow price leads to a "minimum estimate" of the grant element.

2. The Thai government allows goods imported under aid contracts to enter the country free of tariffs and business taxes; hence these transfer payments must be eliminated from our estimates of aggregate consumption costs.[f]

The effects of a loan on the above terms is to lower the aggregate consumption cost rental rate of equipment by about 26 percent for a social discount rate of 15 percent and about 11 percent for a social discount rate of 10 percent. The effects of aid in the form of loans and grants is summarized in columns 5 to 8 of Table 5-2; columns 1 to 4 are repeated from the previous table for the reader's convenience. The important findings may be summarized as follows.

---

[e]For a discussion of the costs of aid to donors and recipients and the effects of variations in the interest charged, grace period, and loan repayment period on these costs, see W.E. Schmidt, "The Economics of Charity: Loans versus Grants," *The Journal of Political Economy*, Vol. 72, No. 4 (1964), pp. 387-95.

[f]It should be noted that provision for tax-free imports of items under aid contract appears to be a voluntary decision on the part of the Thai government; it is not a condition imposed by the aid donor. In any event, even in those cases where aid is extended to cover some portion of local costs, it would not be extended to cover tariffs and taxes.

Table 5-2

**The Average Rate of Technical Substitution Between Labor and Capital, the Ratio of Labor Costs to Equipment Cost at Market Prices, and Aggregate Consumption Costs: Foreign Loans and Grants**

| | ARTS (1) | $\hat{W}^m/\hat{R}^m$ (2) | $\hat{W}^{AC}/\hat{R}^{AC}$ 15% Social Discount Rate (3) | $\hat{W}^{AC}/\hat{R}^{AC}$ 10% Social Discount Rate (4) | $\hat{W}/\hat{R}$ Foreign Loan 15% Social Discount Rate (5) | $\hat{W}/\hat{R}$ Foreign Loan 10% Social Discount Rate (6) | $\hat{W}/\hat{R}$ Foreign Grant 15% Social Discount Rate (7) | $\hat{W}/\hat{R}$ Foreign Grant 10% Social Discount Rate (8) |
|---|---|---|---|---|---|---|---|---|
| 1. Clearing | –.149 | –.169 | –.150 | –.155 | –.202 | –.175 | –.523 | –.539 |
| 2. Grubbing | –.093 | –.120 | –.100 | –.103 | –.135 | –.117 | –.366 | –.378 |
| 3. Excavation Common Soil: 50 m Haul | –.087 | –.128 | –.107 | –.111 | –.144 | –.125 | –.392 | –.402 |
| 4. Excavation Common Soil: 700 m Haul | –.106 | –.165 | –.147 | –.152 | –.200 | –.173 | –.538 | –.553 |
| 5. Excavation Soft Rock: 25 m Haul | –.069 | –.128 | –.106 | –.110 | –.144 | –.124 | –.390 | –.400 |
| 6. Excavation Soft Rock: 700 m Haul | –.089 | –.135 | –.117 | –.120 | –.158 | –.136 | –.415 | –.424 |
| 7. Excavation Solid Rock Drilling & Blasting | –.022 | –.036 | –.030 | –.034 | –.040 | –.038 | –.094 | –.095 |
| 8. Excavation Solid Rock: 200 m Haul | –.114 | –.148 | –.119 | –.124 | –.161 | –.140 | –.438 | –.450 |
| 9. Excavation Solid Rock: 200 m Haul | –.097 | –.151 | –.137 | –.139 | –.184 | –.158 | –.466 | –.473 |
| 10. Embankment | –.135 | –.200 | –.165 | –.175 | –.242 | –.206 | –.670 | –.671 |
| 11. Embankment-selected Material | –.172 | –.200 | –.199 | –.199 | –.254 | –.214 | –.510 | –.518 |
| 12. Gravel Base & Shoulders | –.189 | –.240 | –.199 | –.199 | –.253 | –.215 | –.506 | –.516 |

1. The ratio of the cost of labor inputs to equipment inputs measured at aggregate consumption costs (call it the $\hat{W}/\hat{R}$ ratio) are higher when import content is financed by aid in the form of loans or grants than when import content is financed from local taxation, hardly an unexpected finding. Thus loan or grant finance reverses the tendency for accounting in terms of aggregate consumption costs to favor more labor-intensive methods.

2. The $\hat{W}/\hat{R}$ ratios at aggregate consumption cost are now lower for a 10 percent than a 15 percent social discount rate, the reverse of the case for tax finance where it was found that lower social discount rates favor greater capital-intensity. This reversal is caused by the fact that loans at the stated terms have a significantly larger "grant element" for a 15 percent than for a 10 percent discount rate.

3. Regardless of the social discount rate used, capital-intensive methods involve lower aggregate consumption costs than labor-intensive for *both* loans and grants in every task. In tasks 1, 2, 8, 10, 11, and 12 where the costs of labor-intensive methods were from zero to approximately 10 percent higher than for capital-intensive methods when project costs were financed by taxes, the relative inferiority of labor-intensive methods has increased significantly; the same is true, of course, for all other tasks.

4. When foreign loans are involved and a 15 percent discount rate is used to evaluate the cost of the loan, the desire to minimize aggregate consumption costs would lead to greater capital-intensity than was justified when all costs were tax financed, *and* even greater capital-intensity than would be called for when relative factor costs were measured at market prices (the latter conclusion follows from the fact that the $\hat{W}/\hat{R}$ ratios in column 5 are higher than the corresponding ratios in column 2). That is, given the assumed loan terms and a 15 percent social discount rate, a government seeking to minimize aggregate consumption costs would employ more capital-intensive methods than would a private contractor using relative market prices as his guide.

5. Where a 10 percent social discount rate is employed to evaluate loan costs, the desire to minimize aggregate consumption costs leads to greater capital-intensity than under tax finance and almost as much, and in some cases more, capital-intensity than would be justified when market prices are used to measure costs. That is, in tasks 1, 4, 6, 7, 9, 10, and 11 the relative factor cost ratios in column 6 are greater than in column 2; in the remaining tasks, the relative factor cost ratios at aggregate consumption cost are still below but close to those at market prices. Thus even aid with only a modest "grant element" appears to import a substantial bias toward capital-intensity.

6. Regardless of the social discount rate used (15 percent or 10 percent), grants create a substantially greater bias toward capital-intensity than loans on the assumed terms; the $\hat{W}/\hat{R}$ ratios in columns 7 and 8 are substantially higher than those in 5 and 6. It follows that the greater the "grant element" in the loan (the size of this element depending on both the loan terms and the social discount rate), the greater will be the bias toward capital-intensity.

7. It should be obvious that if governments carry out project evaluations at

market prices alone, making no corrections for "distortions of market prices from real costs" and no attempt to convert costs to aggregate consumption terms, there will still be a substantial bias toward greater capital-intensity, provided governments treat grants of foreign exchange as "free" and loans as equal in cost to the present value of payments of interest and principal; that is, the resulting $\hat{W}/\hat{R}$ ratios in such cases will be higher than those in column 2.

The above arguments are correct as they stand about the direction and magnitude of the bias toward capital-intensity in road construction methods inherent in foreign aid loans and grants. They appear to need no qualification where grants or loans are made to government departments or agencies that will perform the construction activities themselves. Provided that the government carries out a cost analysis such as the one provided in part two of this paper (i.e., following the UNIDO *Guidelines*) or if, as seems more likely in practice, governments carry out a cost analysis using market prices but with grants treated as "free" and the "grant element" in loans correctly accounted for, any agency interested in minimizing costs will choose construction techniques that in most cases are more capital-intensive than would have been justified at relative market prices. The argument appears to need some qualification where construction will be carried out by private contractors (local or foreign) who compete for road construction contracts through competitive bidding. Such contractors would appear to be indifferent about the source of finance by which construction costs are paid. Whether contractors are paid from funds raised by local taxation or from funds provided by foreign loans and grants, the costs they incur are measured in terms of market prices which, as has been shown in the previous section, would lead them to choose capital-intensive over labor-intensive and intermediate techniques in most cases. The bias toward capital-intensity in this case stems from the fact that foreign contractors are able to import equipment (and other materials) free of duty and other taxes, thus reducing equipment costs relative to labor costs.[g] Such tax concessions would appear to be in the interest of the government in terms of minimization of aggregate consumption costs since achieving this goal where foreign loans and grants are involved calls for more capital-intensity in construction techniques than would be called for at relative market prices, but the concessions are a definite disincentive to employment creation.[h] Moreover, it is possible that other biases toward

[g]This concession is granted only on the provision that equipment (and other unused materials) will be reexported within a specified period following completion of the project. It is extended only to foreign and not to local contractors. Thus local contractors operate under a handicap in competing for projects financed by aid.

[h]It might be thought that the desire of governments to increase the import content of a project would be eliminated by the fact that in most cases the size of the loan or grant is based on an estimate of the expected import content of the project made prior to the bidding on the contract and not on the actual import content of the project; i.e., the size of the loan or grant for a project does not vary according to its actual import content. We suspect, however, that the bias remains: in the long-run, donors are not going to be indifferent to the actual import content of projects. To the extent that donors base their estimates of expected import content on the actual import content of similar past projects, it remains in the interest of recipient countries to make sure that the actual import content of projects is as high as possible.

capital-intensity exist in the conditions imposed on bidding for contracts and the contracts themselves. To be eligible for contract award (and sometimes even to bid), a contractor must be acceptable to both the Thai government and the aid donor. The eligibility of each contractor is determined on the basis of past performance and experience on similar work, capabilities in terms of equipment and personnel relative to the requirements called for in the contract, and financial status. These conditions are certainly broad enough to leave room for interpretations that would screen out contractors who would employ more labor-intensive methods. From what we have shown above, such interpretations would be in the interest of a government trying to minimize aggregate consumption costs to the nation. Furthermore, contract conditions regarding speed of completion could rule out labor-intensive methods if, as is commonly thought, they are slower than capital-intensive methods. We have been unable to determine whether contract and bidding conditions affect the choice of technique in practice, but the fact remains that there appears to be substantial scope for this possibility.

There are two methods of eliminating this bias toward capital-intensity inherent in current aid programs. The simplest method would be to continue to tie aid to projects while ceasing to tie it to the import content of projects. That is, donors would agree to finance $X$ percent of any "acceptable" project's costs irrespective of the foreign exchange and local cost content of the project. Since aid is still tied to projects, project evaluators would continue to assess its opportunity cost in the fashion outlined above. However, the costs of all resource inputs would be affected equally since $X$ percent of the cost of any input would be financed by aid, and 100 percent $-$ $X$ percent by local finance, say, taxation, as in our case. Some donors already appear to be making modest steps in this direction by agreeing to cover the import content of projects plus some percentage of local costs. This obviously reduces but does not eliminate the bias since unequal treatment of foreign and local resources remains.

The second way to eliminate the bias toward capital-intensity inherent in current aid programs would be to cease tying aid to specific projects, thus moving from a "project approach" to a "program approach" to aid. Such aid would add to the overall resources available to the economy, but no strings would be attached to the manner in which the aid funds themselves were used. From the point of view of project evaluation, such a change would dramatically alter the calculations of opportunity cost; from the vantage point of a particular project, the opportunity cost of the use of grant funds or loan funds depends on what they would be used for in the absence of the project. The opportunity cost of a grant is no longer zero since, in the absence of the project, these funds could have been used for some other purpose. The opportunity cost of using aid loan funds on a particular project is no longer the discounted present value of the payments of interest and principal since these payments would have to be made even in the absence of the particular project. Thus the opportunity cost depends on what use would be made of the funds in the absence of the project.[i] one must determine the uses to which the funds would have been put: If we value a unit of government consumption at unity (i.e., government consumption), and if the present value of a unit of government investment is greater than one, the appropriate opportunity cost of the use of a unit of foreign exchange in any project is $[(1 + \lambda)(1 - S^G) + S^G P^{\mathrm{GOV}}]$, where $\lambda$ is the premium on foreign exchange and $P^{\mathrm{GOV}}$ is the shadow price of government investment. The value of this expression will be greater than $1 + \lambda$, provided that the government's marginal propensity to save is greater than zero and the shadow price of government investment is greater than one. If such conditions are met, the opportunity cost of a unit of untied aid funds would be substantially higher than that for a unit of tied-aid funds (i.e., a unit of tied-aid funds will always have an opportunity cost of less than $1 + \lambda$, provided the "grant element" in aid is greater than zero). The untying of aid would therefore provide an incentive considerably less capital-intensive than under tied aid.

This recommendation is, of course, not without its limitations. First, project evaluators must correctly perceive the true opportunity cost of untied-aid funds (that this cost is different than for tied funds) and must correctly specify what use would have been made of the funds in the absence of specific projects. This may be hoping for too much. Second, the recommendation opens up all of the well-known donor complaints about the desirability of "program aid" as opposed to "project aid"—that it is hard to evaluate the purposes to which aid is put, that taxpayers in donor countries have nothing (in the physical sense) to show for their money, that recipients lose technical assistance in developing projects which may have a substantial affect on welfare, that donor nations are less sure that their aid is translated into a demand for their own exports, that developing countries are incapable of selecting, constructing, and operating desirable projects without outside pressures to guide them, etc. No doubt there is some merit in these arguments. Nevertheless, one must ask whether the merits inputed to project-tied aid are worth the sacrifice in employment that would correctly measure the social costs of alternative techniques in every type of project, whether identifiable intermediate techniques can be found in road construction, and whether tied-aid is suppressing a potential expansion of employment in other areas besides road construction. Providing answers to these questions would take us far beyond this study, which only represents a modest step in this direction.

[i]It follows, somewhat surprisingly at first, that the opportunity cost of a foreign loan or a foreign grant of the same size is precisely the same from the point of view of the project evaluator. The fact that one requires repayment and the other does not is a matter of indifference; since these funds would have been available whether or not the project under consideration is undertaken, the only relevant opportunity cost is the gains that society foregoes by using the funds on the project rather than elsewhere.

## Discussion: The McCleary Paper

After reviewing his findings for the Seminar group, McCleary closed with two questions. In a social sense, might it be worthwhile to sacrifice some economic efficiency to promote fuller employment and a more equitable income distribution? This, he noted, is a question which only Thais, not aid donors, should try to answer. And second, are there ways of providing aid without a bias toward capital-intensive techniques? McCleary suggested that such a bias could be eliminated if aid were given for programs and not tied to specific projects, so that the opportunity cost of a project to the recipient is not the cost of financing the loan, but rather the value of the next best foregone project. Or the donor could finance a specified percentage of a project without linking the loan directly to the import component of the project.

Several issues relating to this paper were then discussed. The first question asked was how can aid be untied from particular projects? One answer, McCleary responded, would be simply to underwrite a specified portion of a nation's development budget. Or, as he had previously suggested, loans could be made for programs. A participant from a lending agency pointed out that some loans for some types of projects are made to cover foreign exchange costs; but other types of loans closer to those suggested by McCleary can be made at present. However, he continued, the further a lending agency goes away from project loans, the more difficulty it is likely to have with its own government in accounting for the use and effectiveness of aid. Further, if loans were made to supplement a nation's development budget, the donor might require such things as reform of the recipient's tax system. Thus there could be significant costs and even dangers to the untying of aid.

It was noted that shortages of managerial and engineering skills may limit use of labor-intensive methods. How does one feed and house a large number of workers along a rural road project? Decision-making by a local contractor may involve factors other than minimizing cost or maximizing profit, including such things as budget constraints and "connections" with suppliers or subcontractors. In some such cases, the projects may increase income disparities and be of no actual benefit to the people in the rural areas. Foreign contractors prefer to use capital-intensive techniques, because they are most familiar with such methods. It may be difficult or very expensive to enforce a requirement that a contractor use a certain input mix if it is not the most efficient from the point of view of his own self-interest.

There was quite a bit of discussion of methods for determining the appropriate techniques to be used and indeed for selecting the projects themselves. To what extent should local people be consulted; and to what extent should techniques employed and projects undertaken be in accord with local preferences? The dilemma, it was noted, is that major reliance on local preferences may negate the integrated planning function of NESDB. Indeed, NESDB would be caught in a contradiction in trying to calculate meaningful social costs when it must also set national social priorities based on these social costs, because the priorities themselves will in part determine what the opportunity costs are and what the shadow prices should be. The discussion of McCleary's paper ended with an unanswered question: If the Thai government were to undertake road construction projects itself, would it be justified on social grounds in using more labor-intensive methods than the contractors? The answer was not obvious to the Seminar participants.

**Notes**

1. See F.W. Fuchs and J. Vingerhoets, *Rural Manpower, Rural Institutions, and Rural Employment in Thailand* (Bangkok: Manpower Planning Division, National Economic Development Board, 1971) and Chirayu Isarangkun and Nyle Spoelstra, *Some Aspects of Labor Utilization in Thailand* (mimeo; paper presented at the Conference on Manpower Problems in East and Southeast Asia, Singapore, May 22-28, 1971).
2. See Fuchs and Vingerhoets, *Rural Manpower*.
3. Ibid.; and Bevars Mabry and Tanomjit Kompur, *Manpower Imbalances in Thailand 1976 and 1981* (Bangkok: Thammasat University, Faculty of Economics Discussion Paper Series, No. 10, July, 1971); and V. Murali Dhar, *Manpower Supply and Demand in Thailand 1970-1980* (Bangkok: Unpublished M.A. thesis at Thammasat University, Faculty of Economics, February, 1973).
4. UNIDO, *Guidelines for Project Evaluation* (New York: United Nations, 1972).
5. See McCleary, *A Social Cost Analysis*, Chapter 2, Part B.
6. See McCleary, *A Social Cost Analysis*, Chapter 4, Part B.

# Human Resource Development and Foreign Aid: Population Control, Education, and Public Health

**Supachai Panitchpakdi**

> *We have come from the tyranny of the enormous, awesome, discordant machines, back to the realization that the beginning and the end are men; that it is man who is important, not the mission; that it is man who accounts for growth, not just dollars or factories; and above all, that it is man who is the object of all our efforts.*
>
> Pablo Casals (1962)

## Introduction

The human resource is the most important potential source of wealth most developing countries possess. This source is, however, a double-edged sword. If properly developed, it becomes a great asset to a nation (when properly put to use); if not, the development process of the country is thereby retarded, even if the other factors of development remain possible. Genuine development of a nation is heavily dependent on—or more strongly said, equivalent to—the development of the nation's human resources. If this is realized from the start, most problems of development and international aid become much clearer and more comprehensible. If development measures and aid do not combine to better the life of the people in underdeveloped areas through widespread education, health care, and employment, then such measures have obviously failed to achieve their goal, even though their magnitude can be enormous in pecuniary terms. It is probably unnecessary to stress again the unsuitability of income per capita as the indicator of a nation's development. But if this appears like beating a dead horse, then a somewhat cruel note must be added here: that is, the horse is not completely dead.[1]

Although level of income is a convenient measure for making international comparisons, it serves only as one of the minor goals of national economic development. For although the figures of per capita income seem to correlate nicely with the approximate level of poverty or wealth of a country, they do not necessarily indicate the actual direction of causality between higher income and the state of being more developed; the development of the country's human resources comes first, and it in turn generates and sustains a higher level of income. In the economic history of most advanced nations, development of human resources precedes the subsequent higher level of income. For this reason the goals of every developing nation should be set in terms of human units such as literacy rate, life expectancy, unemployment, caloric intake, population per doctor, and urban-rural parity. Although it can be argued that these indicators also correlate with per capita income, aiming at targets set specifically for these indicators can help us obtain a clear view of the main goals of our developmental efforts and particularly of foreign aid. Indeed, if looked at from this angle, it is apparent that several bottlenecks in the process of development occur because priority is given to the wrong projects or to the wrong direction of development. The limit of the so-called absorptive capacity constrains the expansion of investment. The problem of the unemployed educated, observable in many Asian countries, represents an unfortunate waste of scarce resources. The failure of extension services has led to an unusual backlog of knowledge in the agricultural sector—e.g., in the application of fertilizers. The demonstration effect results in copying the style of living and fashion from the industrialized countries which came about in those countries only as a byproduct of the process of modernization and growth without real development. Unless the goals of development in terms of the development of human resources are explicitly accepted and implemented, the process of development will never be completed. What is more, when this potential source of wealth is left undeveloped, it not only remains idle, but actually becomes a burden to the nation. It is therefore hardly a blessing for a country to possess too large a population, especially when only a minor part of that population can be transformed into real human capital.

When these basic premises are accepted, one logically comes to grips with the three essential issues which directly concern human beings, the core of the development process:

a. Containment of the population explosion within tolerable bounds so that potential human wealth does not become a problem,
b. Educational development to transform the potential human wealth into a real asset both in terms of working capacity and cultural and social satisfaction, and
c. Improvement of public health care to prevent a rapid depreciation of the human capital.

These are areas in which each nation must make a major effort, since it can be reasonably expected that external assistance is in a position to contribute relatively little.[2] Yet external assistance in the past cannot be said to have been concentrated in those areas. Future aid to human development should therefore be able to make a far greater contribution, once aims are clearly specified in the above manner, and the assistance is geared to these aims. We shall discuss each of the three issues, first pinpointing the crucial problems at the moment, then suggesting prescriptions and policies to solve these problems, and concluding by considering how external assistance might be useful.

## Containment of the Population

Awareness of this ominous problem in the developing countries has, surprisingly, a rather recent origin. Originally perceived as a real source of wealth even if undeveloped, uneducated, and unskilled, a large population was considered an asset, a sign of power and greatness. But too large an increase in population puts an enormous strain on the resources needed to feed and educate the people sufficiently, resulting in an inability to pursue human resource development. Thailand ranks third highest in the world (after the Philippines and Mexico) in the rate of its population growth. The reasons for this high growth rate are typical of the developing countries. Thailand has experienced a significant reduction in mortality from a fairly constant level of 30 per 1,000 in the mid-1960s. Its fertility has not undergone a similar decline. Between 1960 and 1967, the urban population grew at 4.8 percent annually while the rural population grew at the rate of 3.1 percent. The large proportion of young children in the age structure poses obvious problems (see Table 5-3). For every 100 Thais of working age in 1970, the number of dependents 15 years or under was 89 (compared to 32 in Sweden). This represents a heavy burden which inhibits the improvement of the living standard for many large families.

Because of a higher birth rate in the rural areas, the proportion of youngsters is higher there than in the Bangkok-Thonburi area. The latter has a relatively large proportion of people of productive age, partly due to the immigration of people from the rural areas. This one-way migration has created problems for Thailand's largest urban area in the past and will continue to be a source of unrest in the future if the trend cannot be reversed. Although no explicit data on migration in Thailand are readily available, a survey by the Institute of Population Studies[3] shows that, when change of residence within the metropolis is eliminated from the definition of mobility, a lesser proportion of Bangkok-Thonburi male household heads are classified as mobile than that of their provincial urban counterparts.

**Table 5-3**
**Age Structure in Urban and Rural Areas in 1969-1970 (Percentage)**

| | Rural | | Provincial Urban | | Bangkok-Thonburi | |
|---|---|---|---|---|---|---|
| Age | Male | Female | Male | Female | Male | Female |
| 0-14 | 47.2 | 44.1 | 43.6 | 38.4 | 38.6 | 35.6 |
| 15-59 | 47.2 | 49.4 | 51.0 | 55.0 | 56.2 | 56.9 |
| 60 + | 5.6 | 6.5 | 5.4 | 6.6 | 5.2 | 7.5 |

Source: Visid Prachuabmoh, et al., *The Rural and Urban Populations of Thailand: Comparative Profiles*, Research Paper No. 8, Institute of Population Studies, Chulalongkorn University, 1972, pp. 9-11.

It is mainly because of these problems that the future evolution of the age structure of the Thai population is a matter of great importance. In addition, it has implications for the planning of the educational system and the corresponding labor supply. Any governmental program of human resource development should begin by improving the demographic data that are still far from complete and reliable.[a] Reduction of the fertility rates must be emphasized, since increasing the mortality rate is, of course, undesirable. Analogous to the "autonomous" fall in mortality,[b] the high rate of fertility is to a certain extent autonomous, depending on obscure factors such as tradition, attitude, and value judgements; therefore, reducing it requires determined policy measures. Because of deficiency in birth registrations, determination of fertility rates must be achieved through survey data. Table 5-4 shows the different fertility rates of urban and rural women.

The effort to reduce population growth must be concentrated in the countryside. While marital fertility in Bangkok-Thonburi and provincial urban areas is above levels observed in more advanced countries, information in these areas can be more easily acquired and birth control more easily carried out (see Table 5-5). Moreover, people in rural areas tend to desire a larger-size family than those in urban areas because children can be useful in farm work. This desire makes the reduction of the rural fertility rate more difficult. However, it is apparent from the survey cited[4] that both rural and urban women would reduce the birth rate if they knew of a simple and harmless way to avoid pregnancy.

The success of an official policy to slow down population growth therefore depends primarily on the following three factors.

**Table 5-4**
**Age-specific Marital Fertility Rates, 1969-1970**

| Age of Women | Rural | Provincial Urban | Bangkok-Thonburi |
|---|---|---|---|
| 15-19 | 0.352 | 0.281 | 0.320 |
| 20-24 | 0.418 | 0.352 | 0.342 |
| 25-29 | 0.218 | 0.325 | 0.267 |
| 30-34 | 0.269 | 0.166 | 0.169 |
| 35-39 | 0.211 | 0.124 | 0.089 |
| 40-44 | 0.184 | 0.140 | 0.029 |
| 45-69 | 0.039 | 0.000 | 0.043 |
| 15-49 | 0.263 | 0.193 | 0.165 |

Source: Prachuabmoh, et al., *Rural and Urban Populations of Thailand*, Table 23, p. 62.

[a]Even census data are incomplete. The 1970 census substantially underestimated the population (by some 2 million). Birth registration is generally acknowledged to be deficient.

[b]The fall in mortality is largely autonomous in that it is not connected with any concomitant rise in incomes and levels of living or any other conditions of life, except new medical technology and its applications. See G. Myrdal, op. cit., p. 150.

**Table 5-5**
**Knowledge of Birth Control: Rural and Urban Currently Married Women 15-44**

| | Rural (%) | Provincial Urban (%) | Bangkok-Thonburi (%) |
|---|---|---|---|
| Know Without Reminder | 48.1 | 74.3 | 73.5 |
| Know With Reminder Only | 30.2 | 19.3 | 20.9 |
| Know No Methods | 21.1 | 5.6 | 4.9 |
| No Answer | 0.6 | 0.8 | 0.7 |

Source: Prachuabmoh, et al., *Rural and Urban Populations of Thailand*, Table 33, p. 78.

a. The dissemination of knowledge in rural areas. Not only should informal information be extended to the people through simple media such as posters or folders, but organized education ought also play an important role. Most studies on the relationship between fertility and education point to the fact that the two are inversely related,[5] as they are in the case of Thailand (Table 5-6).

Education has a particularly significant impact among women who have gone beyond the compulsory four-year educational level (as of 1960), although the impact of education on fertility covers all sectors and age groups of the total population.[6] Since the younger segments of the population have been receiving more education, there should be significant changes in the fertility rates in the future (Table 5-7).

b. The inducement of a rational attitude. The desire to have more children should be rationalized through an intensive program of family planning. The attitude demonstrated in Table 5-8 must undergo a substantial shift to make any policy on population worth undertaking.

Historically, Thailand has had a pronatalist policy wherein large families and a high rate of population growth are encouraged. It was not until 1970 that a national population policy was officially declared.[7] Included in the policy is the National Family Planning Program whose main objectives are: (a) to reduce the population growth rate from over 3 percent to 2.5 percent by the end of 1976; (b) to inform and motivate eligible women in family-planning concepts; (c) to make family-planning services readily available throughout the country; (d) to integrate family-planning activities with overall maternal and child health services. This program, and others like it, have resulted in a more equal spread of acceptors through the country, as shown in Table 5-9.

Since 1968, the Thai Budget Bureau has provided a small amount of funding each year as a counterpart of USAID assistance to the family-planning program, and this support will continue. In 1972, for the first time, there were also funds in the Ministry's budget providing specifically for family planning. Significant foreign assistance has been available to family-planning activities in Thailand in addition to that from USAID, from the Population Council, UNICEF, the

**Table 5-6**
**Number of Children Ever Born per 1,000 Ever-married Women by Years of School Completed, by Urban-Rural Residence, 1960 (Standardized for Age and for Total Kingdom by Age)**

| | None | Primary 1-4 Years | Secondary 1-6 Years | University 1 or More Years[a] |
|---|---|---|---|---|
| Bangkok | 3,635 | 3,357 | 3,389 | 1,695 |
| Other Urban, Nonagricultural | 4,232 | 3,810 | 3,314 | 2,729 |
| Urban, Agricultural | 4,488 | 4,371 | 3,615 | 2,011 |
| Rural, Nonagricultural | 3,870 | 3,872 | 3,642 | 1,871 |
| Rural, Agricultural | 4,033 | 3,750 | 3,366 | – |
| | *Total Kingdom* | | | |
| 13-19 | 534 | 488 | 500 | – |
| 20-24 | 1,555 | 1,344 | 1,256 | 700 |
| 25-29 | 2,753 | 2,666 | 2,174 | 1,938 |
| 30-34 | 4,037 | 4,095 | 3,672 | 2,750 |
| 35-39 | 5,288 | 5,300 | 4,402 | 2,444 |
| 40-44 | 6,020 | 5,977 | 4,588 | 3,917 |
| 45-49 | 6,047 | 5,979 | 5,167 | – |
| 50 and over | 5,706 | 5,176 | 3,405 | – |
| Total | 5,061 | 3,270 | 3,231 | 2,403 |
| Total standardized for age | 4,368 | 4,127 | 3,297 | 2,280 |

[a]Limited to women aged 20-44.

Source: Sidney Goldstein, et al., *The Influence of Labor Force Participation and Education on Fertility in Thailand*, Research Report No. 9, Institute of Population Studies, Chulalongkorn University, 1972.

Danish government, and, beginning in 1972, the UN Fund for Population Activities (UNFPA). The International Planned Parenthood Federation (IPPF) provides funding for nongovernmental activites. The majority of governmental funding is for personnel and supplies, while the donor agencies have provided funds primarily for equipment, commodities, supplies, and training. It is striking that, in the field of family planning, relatively small amounts of bilateral aid have been offered compared to the bulk of assistance coming from international organizations. Certainly, therefore, there is room for bilateral aid to expand.

c. The actual application of methods of birth control. Although the preceding two factors are necessary preconditions for population policy to be effective, the actual introduction of the methods and means for limiting fertility finally determines the results. The above preconditions must be brought about mainly

**Table 5-7**
**Percent Literate Females by Age and Rural-Urban Residence, 1960**

| Age | Bangkok | Other Urban, Nonagri-cultural | Urban, Agricul-tural | Rural, Nonagri-cultural | Rural, Agricul-tural | Total Kingdom |
|---|---|---|---|---|---|---|
| 13-19 | 88.2 | 93.6 | 94.6 | 84.4 | 86.8 | 87.0 |
| 20-24 | 83.7 | 88.0 | 90.3 | 77.2 | 79.9 | 80.2 |
| 25-29 | 78.0 | 84.7 | 81.2 | 71.9 | 74.6 | 74.9 |
| 30-34 | 75.0 | 79.9 | 82.6 | 69.7 | 68.2 | 69.4 |
| 35-39 | 68.1 | 68.9 | 76.2 | 51.3 | 47.1 | 50.1 |
| 40-44 | 51.9 | 60.5 | 64.4 | 35.1 | 29.6 | 33.3 |
| 45-49 | 43.7 | 44.3 | 41.0 | 27.1 | 21.5 | 24.6 |
| 50 and over | 29.6 | 24.8 | 24.5 | 9.3 | 6.0 | 8.7 |
| Total standardized for age | 69.6 | 73.0 | 74.1 | 59.7 | 59.3 | 60.6 |

Source: Goldstein, et al., *Influence of Labor Force Participation and Education on Fertility in Thailand*, p. 18.

**Table 5-8**
**Attitudes Toward Having Many Children: Rural-Urban Male Household Heads With Four or More Children**

| Attitude | Rural | Provincial Urban (%) | Bangkok-Thonburi (%) |
|---|---|---|---|
| Advantage | 64.0 | 41.2 | 35.7 |
| Disadvantage | 14.8 | 25.6 | 30.3 |
| Neither | 11.1 | 22.7 | 22.8 |
| Both | 6.2 | 6.1 | 5.6 |
| No answer | 3.9 | 4.5 | 5.6 |

Source: Prachuabmoh, et al., *Rural and Urban Populations of Thailand*, Table 29, p. 78.

**Table 5-9**
**Percentage of Acceptors[a] by Region, 1965-1971**

| Region | 1965-1968 (%) | 1969 (%) | 1970 (%) | 1971 (%) |
|---|---|---|---|---|
| Bangkok-Thonburi | 56 | 27 | 17 | 11 |
| Central | 16 | 14 | 18 | 21 |
| Northeast | 16 | 24 | 27 | 33 |
| North | 9 | 25 | 29 | 28 |
| South | 3 | 10 | 9 | 7 |
| Total | 100 | 100 | 100 | 100 |

[a]Cost per acceptor in Thailand amounted to $8 in 1971 which is among the lowest in Asia (compared to $22 for India, $35 for Indonesia, $14 for Malaysia, and $25 for the Philippines in 1970).

Source: "Family Planning in Thailand 1965-1971," *National Family Planning Program*, p. 24.

by the effort of the authorities in the country itself, with outside aid being supplementary. Inhibitions and false beliefs concerning population policy must be uprooted, requiring a firm and explicit decision by the government to implement birth control as a public policy. Myrdal, entertaining a pessimistic view of foreign aid, emphasizes that "the important thing to stress at this point is that all these things must be accomplished by the governments in the underdeveloped countries themselves. There is indeed very little the developed countries can do by means of aid and technical assistance."[8]

Nonetheless, the following activities seem to need external assistance at this point to render the application effective.[9]

1. Research aimed at perfecting known techniques for birth control, particularly those adapted to the circumstances of the underdeveloped countries.

2. Demographic research. In Thailand, the Institute of Population Studies has done much useful pioneering work in this field.
3. Aid to family-planning programs which does not entail a reduction in aid to other sectors of health care. Blomqvist, adopting the objective of aid programs as that of moving the economy into self-sustained growth as quickly as possible noted: "Since donor countries do not generally seem to be prepared at this time to undertake the relatively large effort required to bring many underdeveloped countries into self-sustained growth, this is a further argument in favor of channelling aid towards assistance in establishing effective programs of population control."[10]
4. Erecting an administrative apparatus that can function well in administering the program of birth control despite the inefficiency of Thai administrative organs in general. Advice from foreign experts who have experience in similar programs might be useful.
5. Establishing effective measures to spread information on birth control into rural areas. In remote areas mobile units must be put to use to reach the local population, and technical aid (medically equipped vehicles) is required to make this possible. Well-equipped mobile clinics with expert guidance and sufficient pamphlets designed in an easily intelligible manner are necessary.

## Development of Human Resources Through Education

One of the pioneering studies on the development of human resources, the Harbison & Myers study,[11] provides a good starting point in a review of the appropriate strategy for countries like Thailand. Although ranking countries according to the level of human resource development represented by the Harbison & Myers composite index leaves much to be desired, the general idea behind the recommended strategy for each group of countries can shed some light on the issue of educational development. Because of the inaccuracy of the composite index, Thailand was ranked as one of the semiadvanced countries, which was a gross overestimation of the country's position at the time (1960). Now, more than a decade later, Thailand seems to be a typical borderline case, between the status of "partially developed" (level II according to Harbison & Myers) and "semiadvanced" (level III). We shall therefore select appropriate measures recommended for both groups of countries and combine them into a set most relevant to the case of Thailand.

It is essential that the number of pupils enrolled and entering primary schools be expanded with all possible speed. But if proper education is to be offered, standards must be improved, attendance made compulsory, and stagnation reduced. The best solution would be to employ only qualified teachers with a secondary education or equivalent. However, the cost of training and employing only such teachers would be prohibitive. The basic problem, then, is to find new technologies of primary education which can be used effectively by low-paid, poorly educated, and unqualified teachers. The application of new techniques such as visual aids, instruction by radio and television, programmed learning, better texts, and simplified curricula may provide a solution. In any case, research and experimentation on educational technology to solve the dilemma of primary education should be given strong support by the government.

The propensity to lavish money on primary school buildings, and to neglect what goes on inside them, should be curtailed. One measure for keeping capital costs of education within limits is to encourage or even require local communities to construct such buildings with their own labor and local materials. Such participation would be an effective means of engendering enthusiasm for education.

A commendable strategy for secondary education should concentrate on improvement in quality and orientation of the secondary schools, rather than simply on expansion to provide more places for primary school leavers. Free secondary education should be available to the best qualified primary school leavers, so that ability to learn can replace ability to pay as the principal criterion for enrollment.

The orientation of general secondary education needs to be changed. Its purpose should be to provide a fundamental and broad education, including adequate exposure to science and mathematics, for students planning to take jobs directly to become technicians or school teachers, or to enter the universities. Therefore, the emphasis should be on multipurpose secondary schools with various choices for specialization, and whose major function would be to produce well-educated people who can later be trained either in employment or in higher education institutes for a wide variety of occupations in the high-level manpower category. This is certainly the most economical means of increasing the quantity, quality, and flexibility of the output of secondary schools.

Shortages of competent secondary school teachers might be met by a program of retraining unemployed college and university graduates to teach such courses as science and mathematics. Traditional teaching methods can be supplemented with new teaching technology, such as educational television for laboratory demonstrations in science. The secondary school bottleneck for further education in scientific and technical subjects may thus be broken at the same time that the problem of the educated unemployed is alleviated.

In terms of numbers, the greatest need is for subprofessional personnel, such as agricultural and engineering assistants, secondary school science and mathematics teachers, agricultural extension workers, community development officers, nurses, and medical technicians. However, without radical changes in the status and pay of the subprofessional occupations, it is doubtful that students will be attracted to them. It would be wise for the government to raise the compensation of the critically needed subprofessional occupations to a level corresponding to that enjoyed by nontechnical university graduates. Without these supplementary measures, building training institutions is likely to be a futile and wasteful undertaking.

Reorientation of higher education is necessary, with more emphasis on scientific and technical faculties, including agriculture, and with relatively less emphasis on humanities, fine arts, and law. Instead of over expanding mass higher education, emphasis should be on quality, since well-trained lawyers, economists, public administrators, industrial managers, and social workers are needed, as are qualified engineers, scientists, and agricultural specialists. To expand all fields, faculties, and universities in equal proportion may be politically attractive, but it is disastrous for strategic human resource development.

However, technical education at the university level costs four to six times as much per student as nontechnical education. Thus the expansion of places for students in technical education, since it may absorb most of the new funds available for university education, may require some curtailment of places in nontechnical faculties. Here it is a clearly suitable gap for foreign aid to fill, should some fields of nontechnical education be found to be relevant to the country and not desirable to contract.

Rural institutions in science and technical fields need to be established and expanded to increase the country's capability to adapt modern science and technology to its own needs. Some research facilities may be established within existing universities.

A comprehensive program for upgrading manpower which is already employed should be established. The need for part-time training and adult education programs is particularly great since so many persons in the high-level manpower category are inadequately qualified. The newly employed secondary school leavers need part-time training to become technicians, and technicians should be able to pursue part-time studies at the university level to attain full professional status.

### *Education in the Third National Economic and Social Development Plan (1972-1976)*[12]

Although national education made progress both in scope and quality during the Second Plan (1967-1971), the ambitious targets set in that plan have not been met. One of the most pressing problems from the Second Plan period was the waste of resources because of the dropouts, failure to pass examinations, and the increasing number of students repeating a course. For primary and secondary education, examination failure rates were 20 percent and 40 percent, respectively. Another problem was that most of the students from primary and secondary schools lacked the experience and skill needed to find suitable jobs after graduation. The Third National Economic and Social Development Plan has placed emphasis on agriculture and rural development, yet no consideration has been given either to improvement of curricula and teaching methods, or to allocation of sufficient funds for educational development. The basic problem which hampers the expansion and improvement of quality in education at all levels is the shortage of qualified teachers. Despite the increased number of teachers during the Second Plan period, shortages are still acute in remote areas where it is very difficult to recruit teaching staff because of low salaries, hard living conditions, and security problems. For higher education in the nonurban regions, in fields such as medical science and agriculture, there are few instructors available. In brief, the following major problems are encountered at different levels of education.

**a. Primary Level.** Shortages of teachers and teaching materials along with the lack of permanent school buildings, especially in remote areas, are the principal problems. These shortages are the cause of deficiencies in the educational system which result in a waste of budget resources. In particular, the student dropout rate at this level is still very high.

**b. Secondary Level (Academic Stream and Comprehensive Schools).** Problems similar to those of the primary level exist. The present system of secondary education is not adequate to meet the requirements for middle-level manpower, and enrollment was lower than the target set for the Second Plan. In the Third Plan, secondary schools will be established in rural areas where such schools do not yet exist, and improvement and expansion of schools near regional universities will be undertaken.

**c. Vocational Education.**[c] The immediate problem is the shortage of qualified teachers, especially in the fields of industrial technology and vocational agriculture. Investment in vocational education requires considerable capital, and supplementary loan projects will be undertaken from the beginning of the Plan period.

**d. Teacher Training.** The qualitative improvement of education at all levels is still below target, partly because the quality of graduates from teachers' training colleges is not up to standard. Lack of instructors, classrooms, and equipment are the main problems.

---

[c]Mark Blaug, along with some others, has serious misgivings about the advisability of expanding formal vocational education, citing the expense and the narrow range of skills provided. ("A Post-Mortem of Manpower Forecasts in Thailand," *Journal of Development Studies*, Vol. 8, October 1971, No. 1, p. 76). Harbison & Myers also voice this concern, (op. cit., pp. 95-96).

**e. Higher Education.** Shortages of instructors in various subjects and of instructors with higher education, and a shortage of Thai and English textbooks are among the most crucial problems. The problems of adult education, vocational, and other special education which did not receive enough attention in the Second Plan, should receive more attention during the Third Plan.

*Blaug's Critique of Educational Planning in Thailand*

Mark Blaug has offered some critical comments on Thai educational plans. His main critique concerns the manpower-requirements approach which has been used to estimate educational needs and which in his opinion contains too many shortcomings to be useful. The following is a list of Blaug's objections that are relevant to consideration of foreign aid.[13]

a. Since the last population census is the one of 1960, there is no reliable information from which trends in labor force characteristics—shifts in occupational structure, changes in industrial occupation, changes in participation rates by sex and age—can be determined. The result is that one must resort to international comparisons which do not necessarily indicate the optimum labor force structure, since not every country involved in the comparisons has planned educational development.

b. No figures have been published in Thailand on employment in the public as distinct from the private sector, much less a breakdown of public employment by educational attainment. The widespread practice of multiple job holding—particularly by civil servants—severely limits the usefulness of data on the occupational and sectoral composition of the labor force in Thailand.

c. The variance around the mean in the Layard-Saigal regressions,[d] as judged by the standard errors of the coefficients as well as by $R^2$'s and the standard error of estimate, is quite considerable, which supports the idea that there is scope for substituting educated manpower within and between occupations, thus weakening the foundations of the manpower-requirements approach.

Blaug offers an alternative planning method: cost-benefit analysis. His findings for Thailand (1970) are summarized in Table 5-10.

The marginal rate of return reflects the rate of return of one grade more of education, while the average rate of return shows the rate of return on the total education received. The following are the main results from this analysis.

Private rates of return are considerably higher than social rates. The private costs of schooling are usually only a fraction of the total resource costs. The largest subsidy seems to have gone to higher education, where direct costs amount to only 18 percent of the social costs.

[d]These regressions relate output per man per sector (cross-section international data) with the occupational and educational characteristics of the labor force by sectors. See P.R.G. Layard and J.C. Saigal, "Educational and Occupational Characteristics of Manpower: An International Comparison," *British Journal of Industrial Relations*, July, 1967.

**Table 5-10**
**Social and Private Marginal and Average Rates of Return, Men and Women Combined, 1970 (Percent)**

| Type of Level of Schooling | Marginal Rate | | Average Rate | |
|---|---|---|---|---|
| | Social | Private | Social | Private |
| 1 | 17 | 26 | 17 | 26 |
| 2-3 | 20 | 34 | | |
| 4 | 27 | 49 | 20 | 38 |
| 5-6 | 14 | 18 | | |
| 7 | 14 | 15 | 17 | 24 |
| 8-10 | 10 | 11 | | |
| 11-12 | 10 | 11 | 14 | 16 |
| 13-14 (Academic) | 7 | 12 | | |
| 13-14 (Teacher Training) | 8 | 9 | | |
| 15 (Academic) | 7 | 9 | | |
| 16 | 7 | 11 | 11 | 13 |

Source: Mark Blaug, *The Rate of Return to Investment in Education: A Report to the National Education Council on the Third Educational Development Plan* (Bangkok: National Education Council, December 1971), p. 5-5.

The highest marginal social rate of return is observed for the lower primary level (P.S. 1-4) and successively higher levels of schooling yield progressively lower rates of return.[e]

The highest social rate (27 percent) is achieved with the completion of P.S. 4. The marginal social rate of obtaining at least some primary schooling (2-3 years) is the second highest rate (20 percent). This pattern suggests that while considerable benefits accrue to individuals who have some primary schooling, the real benefit falls to those who complete the level by finishing P.S. 4. For higher education the private rates do not differ much from those of secondary education.

In terms of social rates, it is found that vocational schooling, whether public or private, yields a lower return than does general academic schooling (8 percent as against 10 percent) due to higher costs not matched by higher earnings among vocational school graduates.[f]

Blaug's principal finding suggests that resources should be shifted toward

[e]This seems to comply with the general proposition in capital theory that continued investment in an activity eventually yields declining rates of return.

[f]A whole series of manpower forecasts in Thailand between 1963 and 1968 led to the conclusion that there were serious shortages of the middle-level manpower in the Thai economy. No mention was, however, made of the appropriate mix of general academic and vocational schools. But preference was given to the expansion of vocational schools.

primary education and away from higher education. This follows from the economic objective of equalizing marginal rates of return in all directions to achieve an optimum allocation of resources. Surprisingly, Blaug's evidence demonstrates that secondary education is not a priority area in terms of economic objectives and that there is even less justification for spending extra funds on vocational rather than general academic secondary schools.

Blaug's study of educational planning in Thailand represents an example of foreign assistance in the form of an expert adviser. While the proper role of the foreign adviser in a developing country has always been a controversial issue,[14] the essence of his study and his long sojourn in Thailand testify to Blaug's knowledge of the Thai educational system. Blaug's results are discussed herein to draw attention to a painstaking exercise carried out by a foreign adviser which deserves to be considered although it may look controversial in some parts. The role of foreign adviser should decidedly be played down in the future but certainly should not be totally rejected. Certain types of advice are still needed, and most developing countries are beginning to appreciate this. The donor countries should, in turn, be more conscientious in providing advice and should prepare advisers to work "with" and not "for" the society and people of the recipient countries.

### *An Essential Program for National Educational Development*

The goal of universal literacy should be stressed in Thailand's program for educational development. Most developing countries begin their educational development program with this basic aim but end up by choosing a seemingly more glorious path of expanding prestigious types of education. In Thailand, primary education, which should have been most emphasized, was more or less neglected between 1966 and 1967 as shown by its declining budgetary share during those years (Table 5-11).

To achieve or approach universal literacy the two following measures must be given priority.

a. A still larger allocation of resources must be given to primary education, especially in the rural areas. This complies with part of the Third Plan, Blaug's recommendation, and Harbison & Myers' recommended strategy. A fitting remark by Myrdal can be added: "There is a fairly general tendency for planned targets for increased primary schooling not to be reached, whereas they are over-reached, sometimes substantially, as regards increases in secondary and, particularly, tertiary schooling. This has all happened in spite of the fact that secondary schooling seems to be three to five times more expensive than primary schooling and schooling at the tertiary level five to seven times more expensive than at the secondary level."[15]

**Table 5-11**
**Educational Expenditure as a Percentage of the National Budget**

| Year | Expense on Primary Education | Expense on Secondary Education | Expense on Other Levels of Education | Total Educational Expense |
|---|---|---|---|---|
| 1965 | 9.6 | 2.0 | 5.5 | 17.1 |
| 1966 | 9.1 | 1.9 | 5.5 | 16.5 |
| 1967 | 7.8 | 1.9 | 5.8 | 15.5 |
| 1968 | 8.3 | 2.0 | 5.5 | 15.8 |
| 1969 | 8.7 | 1.8 | 6.4 | 16.9 |
| 1970 | 9.2 | 1.7 | 6.0 | 16.9 |
| 1971 | 9.9 | 1.9 | 6.3 | 18.1 |
| 1972 | 10.6 | 2.1 | 6.4 | 19.1 |
| 1973 | 10.4 | 2.2 | 6.2 | 18.8 |
| 1974 | 10.4 | 2.2 | 6.6 | 19.2 |

Source: The Budget Bureau.

b. The liquidation of adult illiteracy should be among the most important programs of national development, and such education should take place on a community-wide basis. Adult education should also help to make the school education of children more effective.

It is also true that means have to be found to reduce cost per student at all levels. Buildings do not have to be expensive, especially when materials can be acquired in the locality. And, the rates of wastage have to be lowered. For, although enrollment targets can sometimes be attained, it is not financially feasible to meet the targets for graduates given the average dropout and repetition rates.[g]

Educational quality has to be raised. Some of the steps that should be taken follow.

a. The quality of teachers is low and the student-teacher ratio too high. It has been convincingly shown that generally in Asia, the number and quality of teachers has always been the main bottleneck factor in educational development, and it has worsened over time.[16] The welfare and security of teachers, especially in remote areas, must also be promoted along with their income.

b. The lack of equipment and textbooks depresses educational quality. Incentives to produce textbooks of acceptable quality are needed.

c. Firmer governmental control of educational institutions is needed to prevent private institutions from taking advantage of a large outflow of teachers

[g]H.W. Reiff, "Thailand: The Use of Cost Analysis in Estimating the Total Cost of an Educational Plan and Testing Its Feasibility," in UNESCO:IIEP, *Education Cost Analysis in Action: Case Studies for Planners*, Vol. I, (Paris, 1972) pp. 265-296.

from teacher-training institutes, and from trying to enroll too many students with an inadequate number of teachers.

d. On-the-job training and out-of-school education should be promoted. This kind of training provides opportunities to gain further skill and knowledge particularly for the job in which one is directly involved.

Table 5-12 shows the total educational development expenditures estimated for the Third Plan.

*Educational Development and Foreign Aid*

To be sure, educational development and reform requires mainly the effort of the country itself. In Myrdal's words:

In the educational field there is no real counterpart to the technology of birth control which researchers in the developed countries could experiment with and thus offer to the underdeveloped countries for immediate application. Conditions, and therefore people, are so different in these countries that Western educational experts have very few contributions to make in regard to educational methods.[17]

Although there is some truth to Myrdal's statement, his generalization seems rather crude. In using health and birth control for comparisons, he fails to point

**Table 5-12**
**Educational Development Expenditure by Educational Level, 1972-1976 (Percentage Distribution–Budget Appropriation Only) (Million Baht)**

| Educational Level | 1972 | 1973 | 1974 | 1975 | 1976 |
|---|---|---|---|---|---|
| 1. Primary & Kindergarten | 2,924.18<br>(55.9) | 3,117.12<br>(54.4) | 3,378.18<br>(53.7) | 3,598.22<br>(53.1) | 3,746.87<br>(52.1) |
| 2. Secondary, Vocational, Teacher Training & Higher Professions | 1,169.46<br>(22.4) | 1,383.34<br>(24.1) | 1,552.65<br>(24.7) | 1,655.69<br>(24.4) | 1,729.60<br>(24.1) |
| 3. Higher Education | 878.93<br>(16.8) | 953.89<br>(16.6) | 1,064.59<br>(17.0) | 1,196.90<br>(17.7) | 1,357.96<br>(18.9) |
| 4. Adult and Other Special Education | 254.26<br>(4.9) | 282.42<br>(4.9) | 291.82<br>(4.6) | 324.19<br>(4.8) | 351.73<br>(4.9) |
| Total | 5,226.83<br>(100) | 5,736.77<br>(100) | 6,287.24<br>(100) | 6,775.00<br>(100) | 7,186.16<br>(100) |

Source: *The Third National Economic and Social Development Plan (1972-1976)*, National Economic and Social Development Board, Office of the Prime Minister.

out that, even in these cases, technical assistance alone does not suffice since a much deeper change is required. As we have indicated, changes in attitude and thinking, somewhat like the changes needed for educational development, are required to render birth control effective. Myrdal himself feels that the statement is incomplete since he later adds:

But undoubtedly, foreign assistance specifically aimed at educational reforms could make it possible for the aid giving organizations or countries to exert pressure on underdeveloped countries to proceed more courageously along certain strategic lines in the educational field, provided aid-givers were enlightened enough to want to use such pressure in the right direction.[18]

During the early 1960s, regional targets for educational growth were set for different areas of the world by a series of UNESCO conferences. It turned out later that the high dropout and repeater rates in primary education led to a serious loss of resources and precluded the possibility of meeting the original enrollment targets. The aid donors themselves began to voice concern over the effectiveness of the aid programs. Several meetings of the Development Assistance Committee (DAC) have come to the conclusion that the focus of educational aid should be on improving the effectiveness of the schooling system in developing countries rather than on further expansion. And although the priority training need is still middle-level manpower, greater attention should be given to the need for the "ruralization" of education. It is clear that the past policies of donor countries and agencies regarding educational expansion were aimed at fulfilling the need for qualified manpower. But circumstances have changed in the meantime. The shortages of educated manpower are being overcome, and a general extension into the future of present rates of growth in educational supply will certainly produce new school leavers greatly in excess of the new employment opportunities. Edwards and Todaro entertain this view and observe:

... substantial outside support even for lower levels of education where expansion continues to be justified may simply free national educational resources for the less economically justifiable expansion of higher levels.[19]

With these comments as background, the orientation and content of foreign aid for education in the future can be outlined as follows:

**a. Aid in Financial Terms.** Domestic resources are not sufficient to bring about the desired educational development. Foreign loans and grants (about 5 percent of the total educational budget) are needed as shown in Table 5-13 for the Third Plan.

In the Third Plan there are eighty-four separate programs for education. Just

**Table 5-13**
**Educational Development Expenditure by Source of Funds (Million Baht)**

| Sources of Funds | Amount |
|---|---|
| National Budget | 31,212.00 |
| Foreign Loans | 660.00 |
| Foreign Grants | 1,050.00 |
| Total | 39,922.00 |

Source: *The Third National Economic and Social Development Plan (1972-1976).*

under half of these are directly related to increasing enrollment, and just over half are mainly concerned with increasing the quality and efficiency of existing and new educational institutions. In a recent report by the Ministry of Education, concern is voiced that, despite efforts to control the increase in costs by making greater use of educational facilities and teachers, there will not be sufficient financial resources to implement even the absolutely essential projects, let alone all of the high priority projects.[20] It is thus most likely that considerably more than the originally estimated foreign assistance of 1,710 million baht ($85.5 million) will be needed if both the essential quantitative and qualitative projects are to take place. It can be expected that the sheer internal momentum of the system is likely to use up most of the planned increase in the budget each year of the Plan. Thus if the planned budget is not forthcoming, it is likely that programs for improving quality will be the first to be cut, since quantitative expansion is a political imperative. Therefore, to close this gap, financial assistance should be guided into projects for improving the quality of education, especially in the rural areas. The five most essential projects, from our point of view, that can benefit from external assistance follow.

1. Expansion and improvement of teacher training at the higher certificate and postgraduate levels (Project No. L. 2A). This project is designed to serve the following purposes: meeting the increasing demand for qualified teachers, serving areas having no teacher training at present, and upgrading short-term in-service training courses.

2. Expansion and diversification of M.S. 1-3 (U.S. grades 8-10) in rural areas (Project No. L. 4A). This project aims to open new schools in rural areas that do not have this level of education. The emphasis of the curriculum will be on agriculture, domestic science, and other vocational subjects.

3. Expansion and diversification of regional secondary schools (Project No. L. 4B). This project aims to expand some thirty-eight secondary schools in strategic localities and to diversify the curriculum so that students are oriented towards vocational subjects more in line with future employment opportunities.

4. Development of adult education and functional literacy programs (Project

No. G. 3A). The purposes of this project are: to promote adult education in the more remote rural areas, to produce a special work-text for functional literacy centers, to establish local reading centers in villages throughout the country, to establish fundamental education centers in more remote localities, and to upgrade and reequip adult education supervisory units.

5. Regional in-service training centers (Project No. G. 6A). The objectives are: to expand enrollment rapidly in educationally backward areas, to improve the standard of primary education in remote areas, and to develop supervisory units (educational resources centers) in six regions of the country (three in the South, one each in the North, Northeast, and Southeast).

Table 5-14 summarizes the amount of foreign assistance required for these projects.

**b. External Aid in the Form of Technical Assistance [Apart from Equipment and Experts as Mentioned in (a)].** Such aid can also be a contributing factor in educational development. This type of aid should include the following:[h]

1. Aid in the analysis of the current eduational situation and in the estimation of future trends. This includes lending assistance in the preparation of national educational plans and giving advice on the technique of data collection. Research should also be carried out on the improvement and extension of educational planning as a means of incorporating labor market considerations (more explicitly and practically than hitherto done).

**Table 5-14**
**Foreign Assistance Required, 1972-1976**

| | Proj. I | Proj. II | Proj. III | Proj. IV | Proj. V |
|---|---|---|---|---|---|
| *Loans* | | | | | |
| Buildings | 1,540,000 | 2,600,000 | 560,000 | | |
| Equipment | 2,000,000 | 5,000,000 | 2,340,000 | | |
| Subtotal | 3,540,000 | 7,600,000 | 2,900,000 | | |
| *Grants* | | | | | |
| Experts | 600,000 | | 364,000 | 214,000 | 150,000 |
| Fellowships | 1,607,000 | 1,125,000 | 975,000 | 445,000 | 168,000 |
| Equipment | | | | 695,000 | 170,000 |
| Commodities Paper | | | | 214,000 | |
| Subtotal | 2,207,000 | 1,125,000 | 1,339,000 | 1,568,000 | 488,000 |
| Total | 5,747,000 | 8,725,000 | 4,239,000 | 1,568,000 | 488,000 |

Source: Ministry of Education, "Foreign Loan and Grant Requirements," 1971.

[h]Views supporting these measures are given in OECD: *Development Cooperation* (Paris, 1972).

2. Aid in research and experimentation on innovations in education, especially in the use of appropriate intermediate technologies. Applied research on alternative educational and informational delivery systems should be intensified and expanded.

3. Private international enterprises can also contribute more in training indigenous staff, especially in the tasks of middle-level management. This can help to alleviate the burden of the vocational schools.

**c. The "Brain Drain."** Developed countries should limit the free inflow of skilled and educated migrants from developing countries. Although it is still undecided whether or not the "brain drain" is a serious problem for Thailand, to a large extent judgment on this issue involves the judge's personal standpoint and development philosophy. Although Thailand has not visibly suffered from the "brain drain" problem—as some other countries in Asia have—the long sojourn of quite a few Thai doctors abroad has meant substantial losses not only in terms of the official investment in their studies and taxation, but also in terms of the improvement of public health care (opportunity costs) that could further human resource development. Therefore, as a kind of aid to the developing countries, developed countries should check immigration of professionals from the former. If not stemmed, the "brain drain" could easily become another significant problem for Thailand's human resource development policy, especially since the number of Thai students studying abroad is rapidly increasing.

**d. Scholarship Assistance.** The donor countries offering scholarships should be more strict and more specific with this form of aid. This does not mean that the goal of selection has to be an even more accurate identification of the cream of the country's manpower. On the contrary, stipends should be increasingly directed towards that group of people—not likely to come into consideration because of circumstances, such as living in remote areas or not working in some strategic offices or ministries—who can truly benefit from the training and whose activities are directly relevant to the nation's economic development. In the past, too many scholarships ultimately fell into the hands of those who were not really interested in the fields covered by the fellowships but accepted them because of the chance to travel abroad and a likely promotion when they came back. Domestic authorities who supervise the distribution of scholarships sometimes offer them to their own people first, a sordid business that has become a common practice in Thailand. It would be much more profitable to the recipient country if the donor country would specify exactly what kind of people they would like to provide with this form of aid. The standards to be used in giving scholarships should not be based on intelligence and high qualifications alone; instead they should be based on the strategic role of the recipients. Moreover, the language barrier need not be prohibitive, since mastering simple technologies depends mainly on watching and imitating the demonstration. And, for that matter, these scholarships do not have to finance training abroad, but could be used for training in the capital city or at one of the domestic educational centers.

## Improvement of Public Health Care

There is strong evidence confirming the relationship between working capacity and the nutrition and health of manpower. H. Correa, among others, has convincingly shown that there exists a relationship between income and the intake of nutritive elements, with the intake of calories stabilizing at around 3,000 calories per day.[21]

To promote human resource development, educational development is wasted if it does not go hand in hand with the improvement of public health care. The major obstacle to public health development in Thailand is a personnel shortage, especially of physicians and nurses in rural areas. The ratio of physicians to population in the Bangkok-Thonburi area is 1 to 1,400, whereas in the rural areas it is 1 to 10,000. Even in the rural areas, physicians tend to be concentrated in towns, making the lack of medical care in remote areas even more acute. Apart from many shortcomings beginning with the Thai authorities themselves—e.g., at a time when there is an acute shortage of certain types of medical personnel, physicians are foolishly posted as institution chiefs and burdened by excessive administrative duties—there are other gaps foreign aid can advantageously be used to fill, among which are the following.

a. When more doctors and nurses are trained, steps should be taken to draw this much-needed manpower to the rural areas. Among the incentives to attract these doctors and nurses should be compensation in terms of extra income and amenities. Also, the availability of appropriate equipment and standardized medical centers equipped to fight specific diseases of the areas would be additional incentives. Foreign aid allocated to health centers should be increasingly concentrated on the attempt to bring about these conditions.

b. Doctors and nurses should not be lured away by attractive offers from abroad. As already suggested, limiting these offers alone could be a great aid to public health development in Thailand, since matching such offers financially is impractical.

c. If scholarships are to be given, it is most appropriate to offer them to train additional practical nurses, health workers, and dental hygienists, since, as admitted in the Third Plan, it is this category of personnel which will be most needed in assisting rural physicians.

d. Medical analysis and research are not sufficiently encouraged by Thai authorities. In the past, research has largely depended on foreign assistance. Considering the importance of medical research, aid for this purpose should be stepped up in the future.

Table 5-15 summarizes the funds allocated for public health improvement in the Third Plan. Relative to the need, these funds are likely to be on the low side.

e. Although Thailand has a comparatively abundant supply of food, malnutrition due to a lack of knowledge of the nutritive values of food or to a failure to select a balanced diet, among other factors, is still a problem.[22] The corn-soya milk blend (CSM) and the wheat-soya blend (WSB) which have been available for some years through UNICEF provide an improvement in protein intake. Such programs are a significant contributing factor to public health development and should be intensively pursued in the future. It is intended, through educational campaigns, to inform the public of the importance of sound nutrition. The FAO/WHO Interregional Training Course in Fundamentals of Nutrition and Their Application was once conducted in Thailand. Such courses should be conducted more often in the future through the help of international organizations.

f. In connection with the preceding remark, it is to be expected and recommended that in the future more and more joint research for the Southeast Asian region will take place. The Project of Tropical Medical and Public Health (TROMED), for example, has pooled the resources of the participant countries in a cooperative endeavor to develop and upgrade the research and training capability of the existing facilities in these countries. Foreign aid to such institutions can thus produce results applicable and available to a large community.

## Concluding Remarks

External assistance can do much to promote development if development targets are clearly spelled out in terms of the betterment of human life. In the past, too

**Table 5-15**
**Budget Allocation for Public Health (Million Baht)**

| Source | Total |
|---|---|
| 1. Regular Government Budget | |
| 1.1 Ministry of Public Health | 5,500.00 |
| 1.2 Outside the Ministry | 160.58 |
| 2. Other Budgetary Categories | |
| 2.1 Public Health Assistance Funds of the Municipalities | 32.50 |
| 2.2 Foreign Financial Assistance | 840.00 |
| Total | 6,533,08 |

Source: *The Third National Economic and Social Development Plan (1972-1976).*

much thinking about aid has been done purely in pecuniary terms, and the results have correspondingly been disappointing. Transfer of "capital," in the sense of finance, does not necessarily result in a transfer of real resources or capital in the physical sense of capital goods. Joan Robinson goes even further to suggest that "a country which receives an inflow of finance is not receiving a supply of a factor of production called 'capital': it is enjoying the possibility of running a surplus of imports or amassing monetary reserves."[23] If this paper leans too heavily toward discussion of the form and content of aid programs, it is precisely because of an awareness of this deficiency. If we are really determined to render foreign aid useful in the future, we should first concern ourselves with the analysis of the existing gaps which foreign assistance can help to fill. The backlog of problems in the development of human resources is such a gap and an important one since it is essential to the entire development process. We have attempted to demonstrate that well-thought-out programs of foreign aid can perform a significant auxiliary function in supplementing the national effort. Although the development of human resources basically requires the kind of reform which can only be effected by local authorities, foreign aid can do much to accelerate this process. For example, if the government opts for quantity for political reasons, the quality gap should be bridged by external assistance; but only, of course, if this gap concerns only human and physical inputs and not a change in the structure of the system. Hopefully, the discussion of the desired direction of aid provided by this paper can improve development cooperation.

## Notes

1. I. Adelman and C.T. Morris, *Society, Politics and Economic Development: A Quantitative Approach* (Baltimore and London: The Johns Hopkins Press, 1971), Table IV-5, p. 170.

2. Gunnar Myrdal, *The Challenge of World Poverty: A World Anti-Poverty Program in Outline* (Baltimore: Pelican Books, 1970).

3. Visid Prachuabmoh, et al., *The Rural and Urban Populations of Thailand: Comparative Profiles*, Research Paper No. 8, Institute of Population Studies, Chulalongkorn University, 1972, pp. 21-23.

4. Visid Prachuabmoh, et al., *Rural and Urban Populations of Thailand*, Chapter 7.

5. David M. Heer, "Educational Advance and Fertility Change," International Population Conference, London, 1969, Vol. III.

6. Sidney Goldstein, et al., *The Influence of Labor Force Participation and Education on Fertility in Thailand*, Research Report No. 9, Institute of Population Studies, Chulalongkorn University, 1972, p. 25.

7. "Family Planning in Thailand 1965-1971," *National Family Planning Program*, Ministry of Public Health, Thailand (1972 edition).

8. Myrdal, *The Challenge of World Poverty*, p. 165.

9. Some of these aids are also admitted by Myrdal to be useful.

10. A.G. Blomqvist, "Foreign Aid, Population Growth, and the Gains from Birth Control," *Journal of Development Studies*, Vol. 8, October, 1971, No. 1, p. 17.

11. F. Harbison and C.A. Myers, *Education, Manpower and Economic Growth: Strategies of Human Resource Development* (London: McGraw-Hill Book Company, 1964).

12. *The Third National Economic and Social Development Plan (1972-1976)*, National Economic and Social Development Board, Office of the Prime Minister, Bangkok.

13. Blaug, "A Post-Mortem of Manpower Forecasts in Thailand."

14. Adam Curle, *Planning for Education in Pakistan* (London: Tanstock Publications, 1966), p. 2.

15. Myrdal, *The Challenge of World Poverty*, p. 188.

16. See S. Panitchpakdi, *Educational Growth in Developing Countries: An Empirical Analysis* (Rotterdam: Rotterdam University Press, 1973).

17. Myrdal, *The Challenge of World Poverty*, p. 208.

18. Ibid., p. 209.

19. E.O. Edwards and M.P. Todaro, "Educational Demand and Supply in the Context of Growing Unemployment in Less Developed Countries," *World Development*, Vol. I, No. 384, March/April 1973, pp. 107-117.

20. Ministry of Education, "Foreign Loan and Grant Requirements of the Ministry of Education during the Third Five Year Plan Period 1972-1976" (Bangkok, 1971).

21. H. Correa, *The Economics of Human Resources* (Amsterdam: North Holland Publishing Company, 1967). See Chapter 4.

22. "Public Health in Thailand," Ministry of Public Health (Bangkok, 1968).

23. Joan Robinson, "The Need for a Reconstruction of the Theory of International Trade," in *International Trade and Money* M.B. Connolly and A.K. Swoboda, eds. (London: George Allen and Unwin Ltd., 1973) pp. 15-25.

# Discussion: The Supachai Paper

Supachai's presentation of his paper included a strong plea for development strategies aimed at development of human resources rather than such things as infrastructure, industrialization, and per capita gross national product. The human capital potential of developing countries is as yet unrealized. Supachai discussed and endorsed a concern articulated by Barbara Ward (Lady Jackson) in which she had contended that an obstacle to further aid is a growing concern that aid has not worked. There are more people in the world who are worse off now than was the case at the beginning of economic development efforts after World War II. The developing countries have tried to imitate what the developed countries had done; but not enough attention has been paid to the facts that the developed countries had industrialized slowly and that average education levels and agricultural productivity had grown apace with industrialization.[a] There is need to improve human skills and agricultural productivity in developing countries. Further, human capital should be developed for its own sake. Education which broadens people's horizons, raises their cultural level and increases their social satisfactions is a valuable consumption good as well as an investment.

Supachai viewed population control and education as closely tied to each other, since the basic problem in population control is dissemination of information to rural areas, and since there is strong evidence that educational levels are inversely related to fertility. But education has such an impact only on women who have gone beyond the four years now required in rural Thailand. These four years, by themselves, make virtually no difference. One cause for optimism, Supachai observed, is that the government is now stressing education of females in both rural and urban areas, and in the future the Thai population will contain a larger percentage of women who have gone further in their schooling. Education in family planning must go beyond availability and use of birth-control devices, since many people in rural areas want large numbers of children—and for good reason in a social structure in which the family is an economic unit providing support for the aged and incapacitated.

Immediately following Supachai's presentation, the question was raised as to whether education really lowered fertility or whether both education and lower fertility might be associated with more fundamental aspects of the social and economic structures. Thailand's family-planning program was then discussed at some length, and several problems with it were noted. A survey by NESDB suggests that the program may have been too much oriented toward a medical approach; that there has been poor coordination between medical and promotional teams; that statistical studies of the effectiveness of the program were poorly designed and gave incorrect results; and that people were treated rudely

[a]See, e.g., *The Lopsided World*, (New York: Norton, 1968).

and inconsiderately at the clinics. Cultural norms were violated in instances such as the use of male doctors in Muslim areas. Family planning, it was argued, must be multidisciplinary and closely tied to educational and fiscal policies. The latter are important: The tax structure and the public spending systems should not encourage large families. In the nation's Third Plan (1972-1976), population policy is limited to family planning; but in the future Thailand's policy must expand to embrace aspects of health, education, delivery systems, and coordination between private and public programs. Aid donors should consider the need for this sort of integration.

Puey raised several questions regarding Supachai's paper. He did not think Supachai should have accepted Professor Blaug's cost-benefit analysis of higher and vocational education programs.[1] Cost-benefit analysis does not give any positive weight to the accumulation of knowledge in universities nor to the value of the research role of universities. A lack of understanding of the history of vocational education in Thailand, particularly its rapid and ill-conceived expansion during the Phibun regime (1947-1957), may have misled Blaug. Vocational education in agriculture is too new to evaluate properly. And if cost-benefit analysis yields an unfavorable evaluation of vocational education in trade and industry, the problem may lie in the failure of the economic system to have industrialized rapidly enough to absorb vocational education graduates no matter how well trained. Puey called attention to informal and adult education programs which have not been studied and which he believes would prove to have very favorable cost-benefit ratios.

Puey then turned to problems of prenatal and child care. The quality of the future population begins with prenatal care, he observed. And adequate nutrition after birth, particularly in the first two years, is absolutely crucial to a child's mental as well as physical development. Children need parental attention and concerned care but often do not get them in Thai society, where grandmothers and aunts may care for children while the parents work. There is little that foreign donors can do to influence Thai patterns of child care, but there is one area in which foreign assistance might be very helpful. Often in Thailand, the family environment is not conducive to encouragement of children to read. Worse still, Thai television, which children do watch, is "a lot of trash." Indeed, the kind of television programming children in Thailand are exposed to is antieducational. Foreign aid might play a very important role in effective use of the mass media, especially in the development of educational programming for television.

In reply, Supachai stated that he agreed with Puey except that he would want to distinguish among types of vocational education. Some vocational education was good and effective; but industrial vocational education was expensive and not a good investment if graduates did not match the industrial needs of the country. He asked why general secondary education with some vocational components might not be just as effective, with industrial firms providing on-the-job training to graduates. Finally, he pointed out that the fact had to be faced that illiterate adults were just as employable as literates in many rural occupations.

One participant argued that there was no alternative to the use of cost-benefit analysis in educational planning because the statistical base was too poor to permit use of manpower planning and forecasting, which might otherwise be a preferable approach. It was argued that the quality of teachers and of the training in teacher-training institutes was so low that many private schools would not employ graduates of these institutes. Vocational education in agricultural subjects is often taught by teachers with no practical experience in farm work. It was noted that municipal financing, controlled by the national government, is so stringent that even the city of Bangkok is unable to provide decent primary education. On the other hand, teaching loads in universities and medical schools, in the opinion of one participant who is himself a professor, are scandalously low.

Another participant strongly endorsed Puey's comments on Thai television, going even further and describing it as conveying "poisonous" social values. Aid donors could make a significant contribution by helping to develop educational television, he continued; but the Thai government itself simply must do something about the present ownership and administration of both television and radio stations.

In a concluding remark, it was noted that NESDB and the Thai government had to resolve the controversy over use of cost-benefit analysis in education, since the issue is basically one of values. If the goal is investment in human capital for productivity purposes, then cost-benefit is appropriate. But if the goals are social and cultural, then the cost-benefit ratio is irrelevant and standards such as the literacy rate must be used. In any event, Thais and not donors have to resolve this conflict.

## Note

1. M. Blaug, *The Rate of Return to Investment in Education: A Report to the National Education Council on the Third Educational Development Plan* (Bangkok: National Education Council, December, 1971). See also "A Post-Mortem of Manpower Forecasts in Thailand."

# Direct Foreign Investment in Thailand

**Sura Sanittanont** and **Twatchai Yongkittikul**

## Introduction

Private foreign investment has undoubtedly played, and will continue to play, an important role in the economic development of many developing countries in Asia with open economies. Broadly speaking, foreign investment may be expected to benefit host countries in the following areas: (1) It should result in the immediate expansion of national production, either for domestic consumption or for exports; (2) it may generate employment in the host countries to the extent that foreign investments flow into the developing countries to take advantage of cheap labor resources; (3) it is a source of foreign exchange; and (4) perhaps more importantly, it has the potential to serve as a vehicle for technological transfer through which new and more efficient production techniques and management know-how can be transmitted from the developed countries to the developing host countries.

However, the overall economic benefits of foreign investment to a particular host country are by no means uniform or automatic. In fact, the social costs of certain foreign investment projects may well exceed the social benefits accruing to the host country. Apart from the usual economic cost and benefit considerations, foreign investment can produce important externalities in terms of social and cultural impacts, which may not always be desirable. Wealth and income distribution in the society, for example, are significantly affected by the quantity and quality of foreign investment. Moreover, ways of life and patterns of social values can also be significantly altered. In assessing the quality of foreign investment, one should therefore bear in mind that in many ways the economic and sociocultural effects of foreign investment are interrelated.

While the positive economic effects of foreign investment on a developing country in the short-run are widely acknowledged, whether the long-run economic effects are generally positive has remained a subject of great controversy. While proponents of foreign investment enthusiastically propound its advantages, opponents cite the disadvantages and ill-effects of foreign investments with equal vigor. There is validity in the arguments of both sides, as there are gains as well as losses in opening one's door to foreign investments. Whether the host country comes out a net beneficiary or a net loser depends on the effectiveness of the administrative machinery that is responsible for attracting, screening, and controlling the operations of such investments. If a country can attract good projects and weed out poor ones—both from the private and societal points of view—then it stands to benefit from foreign investments.

Thailand has been pursuing a very liberal policy towards foreign investment since the early 1960s, offering various tax concessions and other incentives to foreign investors. Yet, the performance of foreign investment in Thailand seems to be less than impressive from the perspective of overall economic development as well as when compared with its role in such neighboring countries as Singapore and Malaysia. This paper proposes to make a brief investigation into the role and performance of foreign investment in the Thai economy. Policy recommendations are also advanced as guidelines to improve the quality of foreign investment in Thailand.

## Some Salient Features of Direct Foreign Investment in Thailand

Foreign investment in Thailand prior to 1960 was insignificant in volume. The small amount of foreign capital that did flow in was channeled to relatively limited areas of operation including mineral extraction, rubber plantations, teak processing, and the production of simple consumer products.

In 1960, the government promulgated the Industrial Investment Promotion Act as part of a policy to accelerate economic growth. Under this act, various incentives in the forms of import duty exemptions and income tax holidays are granted to local and foreign investments. Since that time, foreign investment has increased enormously and has assumed an important role in the industrial development of the country. It has also become a major component in Thailand's balance of payments, working as an important offsetting factor to a chronic and huge balance-of-trade deficit. However, the volume of direct foreign investment tends to fluctuate quite markedly from year to year.

About half of the promoted investment projects have taken the form of joint ventures with local partners. The percentage of promoted firms owned solely by foreign investors has declined rapidly; and in recent years the number of promotional certificates issued to such firms has been negligible. Evidently, foreign investors have found it politically wise to have local partners in their ventures in the face of rising public resentment against what is viewed as foreign economic domination.

In terms of equity participation, foreign capital now constitutes roughly one quarter to one third of total registered capital, but with a visibly declining trend in recent years. It should be pointed out, however, that the relatively minor share of equity participation by foreign investors does not reflect the actual influence wielded by foreign investors in the joint-venture enterprises in which they participate. Foreign partners typically hold key management positions in an organization, usually with voluntarily inactive local partners holding unimportant positions. The Japanese are the largest single group of foreign investors in Thailand, accounting for more than one third of the registered foreign capital, with Americans, who account for about 16 percent, ranking second. The Chinese from Taiwan and the Europeans are the other major investors in Thailand.

Of the 680 investment projects that have enjoyed promotional privileges, 59 percent or about 400 projects have been concentrated in five major industrial groups, namely, textile and fiber products, food and cold storage, metal and its related products, hotels, and wood products. These account for 60 percent of the total registered capital. Among these major industries, Japanese equity participation is significant in metal and mineral product industries.

Among the most notable features of the pattern of foreign investment in Thailand, from the point of view of understanding and evaluating the effects of this type of investment on the economy and society as a whole, are the following.

1. Investment tends to concentrate in the vicinity of Bangkok, where infrastructural facilities are far more developed than in the outlying rural areas.
2. Most of the investments are in capital-intensive, import-substituting industries producing primarily for the city. In recent years, there has been heavy investment in the textile industry for export.
3. Due to the nature of the incentive program provided by the government, many of the industries are relying on imported raw materials as well as imported capital equipment, utilizing local cheap labor as the main local input. Food-processing industries are the major exception.

To be fair to foreign investors, it should be pointed out that locally owned and financed investment projects generally exhibit roughly the same characteristics.

## The Public View and Attitude Towards Foreign Investment

The attitude of the general public towards foreign investment has deteriorated in recent years. During the 1960s, foreign investments and foreign businessmen were quite warmly welcomed. The economic boom of the 1960s and the favorable government policy toward foreign investment resulted in an unprecedented influx of foreign investment, especially from Japan. But within a year after what appeared to be the end of the economic boom, demonstrations led by university and vocational students began to erupt with increasing frequency and intensity, culminating in the "violent" demonstrations against the visiting Japanese Prime Minister in January, 1974.[a] Since then, demonstrations have become widespread and have come to include protests against alleged American

[a]Only by Thai standards could these demonstrations be called violent. Paper models of Japanese cars were burned instead of real ones and material damage was confined to a few broken windows.

interference in this country's internal affairs. Now demonstrations have been taken up by hotel workers, factory workers and even farmers against low wages, poor working conditions, and high rent and interest. The current labor unrest can be regarded as a confrontation between labor and the owners and management of various enterprises, Thai and foreign alike.

These expressions of resentment toward foreign investment and foreign economic "domination" are in fact expressions of public disenchantment with the overall pattern of economic and social development of the country. After more than a decade of governmental development efforts, income disparities between the rich and the poor, as well as between the urban and the rural sectors, have been widening at an alarming rate. Foreign investments, as the mass of the people see them, have contributed to and even accentuated this anomalous pattern of economic growth. Foreign business and foreign investments, being the most conspicuous symbols of economic disparities, have become convenient targets for public dissatisfaction with the country's economic structure. This widespread discontent and frustration over economic conditions led to angry public demonstrations in October, 1973, which eventually toppled the military regime that had ruled the country. Since then, social unrest, labor disputes, rampant inflation, and ensuing political and economic instability in the country have severely damaged the investment climate in Thailand. The precise extent to which foreign investments have been discouraged cannot yet be determined, but it is generally agreed to be significant. This will have very far-reaching consequences on the economic conditions of Thailand in the medium-term future. Unless the current social and economic instabilities are dampened, and unless the country's basic policies toward foreign investment are clearly defined, Thailand should not plan to rely on foreign investment to play any significant role in the country's industrialization.

Before examining ways and means of improving the investment climate, it is necessary to look into the underlying causes of discontent with foreign investments among the Thai people. There are two levels of discontent, or resentment, toward foreign investments. First, on the people-to-people level, there is an apparent lack of harmony between the Thai people and businessmen, on the one hand, and foreign investors and businessmen residing in Thailand, on the other. One of the major complaints among the Thai people about foreigners, and particularly about the Japanese who are forming an increasingly conspicuous economic presence in Thailand today, is that some of them possess an exaggerated sense of superiority and tend to be a socially closed group living in a foreign enclave in this country. A lack of communication and understanding naturally breeds suspicion and resentment. To build up harmonious economic and cultural relations between the two peoples, both the local people and the foreigners must try to understand each other and adjust themselves in whatever way they can to accommodate the other. With proper orientation of foreign businessmen to the ways of the host country and open mutual exchange, the situation can certainly be improved markedly.

A more complicated and difficult problem in interpersonal relations is that Thais often feel that foreigners who come to do business in this country benefit more from their ventures or joint ventures than do the local people or local partners. However, the fact must be faced that foreign investors usually can manage to get a larger share of the benefit from any venture even when they are "playing a clean business game," because foreign businessmen are often better equipped, better trained, better financed, and more skillful than their local counterparts. In other words, the relationship between foreign investors and local investors is a strong-partner weak-partner relationship. Naturally, the strong partner will always come out ahead, unless he can voluntarily restrain himself from taking full advantage of his position. However, it is unrealistic and difficult to expect businessmen, foreign or Thai, to exercise such self-restraint. Local businessmen will have to learn from experience and train themselves to catch up with their partners in this game. This will be a long and costly process.

Second, there has been a growing feeling among educated Thais that foreign investments are not making the positive contributions to the industrialization and overall economic development of the country that are expected of them. In the most crucial area of technological transfer, for instance, it is felt that after more than a decade's history of industrial promotion and the influx of foreign investments, very little impact has been made on the overall productivity of the country. This is attributed primarily to the fact that foreign investors are reluctant to train and put Thai people in important technical or managerial positions. Furthermore, it is maintained that whatever technological transfer has been effected, the benefits have been confined to only a small group of people (namely the Thai members of joint-venture projects) in the urban sector, thereby contributing to the widening gap between the rich and the poor, and between the rural and the urban sectors.

## The Need for a Foreign Investment Policy

From the foregoing brief analysis of foreign investment in Thailand, it is apparent that the government must make a critical reassessment of past policies and practices regarding foreign investment policy for the present and the future.

First and foremost, the government must decide whether or not Thailand will continue to allow foreign investment to play a role in the industrialization of the economy, and if so to what extent. Considering the present economic structure, resource endowment, and the level of technological development of the country, it seems fairly certain that Thailand will continue to rely on foreign investments in the forseeable future, unless there is a sudden and dramatic change in the country's basic political and economic policies, which is rather unlikely. This being the case, the government must proceed to clarify its position publicly. At present, foreign investors must be quite confused as to whether they are welcome in Thailand. On the other hand, government agencies concerned with attracting and promoting foreign investment are trying to do their part in getting as much foreign investment as possible. Local businessmen are also trying to attract foreigners to enter into joint-ventures with them. On the other hand, certain other public regulatory agencies and a large part of the vocal public often criticize foreign investments as exploitative, calling for the government to discourage or even ban foreign investment; and radical voices are occasionally heard calling for nationalization of foreign businesses.

It is apparent that the conflicting sentiments and pronouncements against foreign investments are very damaging to the investment atmosphere in the country, despite the fact that Thailand possesses many attractive features for foreign investment—e.g., rich natural resources, low wages, and a very versatile labor force. Some foreign investors liken the situation of Thailand to that of a very beautiful maiden with many young men courting her, but with uncooperative parents who tend to drive away potential suitors. Therefore, the government must first develop a clear and coherent policy of its own toward foreign investment, and it must then convince the public of its correctness and importance if it does decide to attract foreign investment.

The second major area in which improvement requires government action has to do with cumbersome laws, and confusing and conflicting laws, and procedures governing investors and foreign investments. Foreigners are concerned and discouraged, for instance, by the Alien Business Law and the Alien Occupation Law. The difficulties arise not merely because such laws exist, but because of their unclear definitions and inefficient and costly procedures. Foreigners may have to wait for months before a ruling as to whether they will be allowed to participate in a certain line of business. They may have to wait for months before they receive the necessary work permits. And while waiting, expenses must be paid. These factors often weigh more than, or just as much as, any tax concessions received by foreigners. It is through efficient practices regarding foreign investment that Singapore has made itself such an attractive and popular place for foreign investment.

The above improvements, when implemented will encourage *more* foreign investments to be made in Thailand but not necessarily *better* ones from both the private and societal points of view. Yet, it is a better quality of investment projects that this or any country needs. This means that we must try to attract projects with quite different features and characteristics from most that we have been able to attract so far. We need to attract foreign investments that will effect significant transfers of technology, both in the technical and in the managerial fields. Such transfers of technology should not be confined to a small group of people. The knowledge should be diffused among the masses. However, it is the responsibility of the government more than that of the foreign investors to see to it that the technological level of the masses is raised. Foreign investments should also be directed to the less-developed parts of the country, rather than to

Metropolitan Bangkok. Labor-intensive, employment-generating projects should be encouraged rather than capital-intensive ones. Finally, in view of the country's huge and chronic balance of trade deficits, export-oriented projects should be given priority over projects that produce goods for local consumption, since the latter may be "new" consumer items rather than substitutes for imported consumer goods.

Only when we can attract such "quality" foreign investments will it be in the long-term interest of this country to open its door to foreign investment. And only when we have succeeded in doing so will public resentment and hostility towards foreign investments and businessmen be eliminated.

It is not always necessary for Thailand to give greater concessions in terms of taxes and other benefits to attract more and better foreign investment. The rate of return to investment in Singapore is generally lower than in this country. And yet Singapore is generally rated as having a better investment climate despite the limited resources and markets of that country. Clarity and stability of government investment policy, and efficient administrative processes are highly valued in foreign investors' minds. In short, certainty in policy, stability in the investment atmosphere, and simplicity in administrative practices weigh heavily in potential investors' decisions to invest.

Probably the most important thing to be done to attract more foreign investment to Thailand and to improve its quality is a total revamping and substantial improvement of the administrative agency concerned with attracting and screening foreign investment, the Board of Investment (BOI), because it is this agency and the officials working in it that make it possible or impossible for Thailand to attract more and better foreign capital. Objectives can be set, and criteria can be laid down, but unless there are people competent and concerned enough to execute them, the objectives will remain on paper.

It is not possible to reform the entire administrative system in this country in the near future; and if the agency responsible for foreign investment remains a part of the existing administrative system, it will not be able to escape the red tape and the drawbacks of the system. The low salary scale imposed by the civil service alone is sufficient to make it impossible to recruit and retain administrative personnel at BOI who possess the required vast knowledge and skill, both managerial and technical. Therefore, the short-run solution to this problem is to spin off BOI from the civil service system of the country and accord it an autonomous status as has been done in some other countries. Unless such a drastic step is taken, there can be no escape from the vicious circle of poor organization, poor administration, and miserable performance.

## Conclusion

Foreign investment has played a significant role in the industrialization of the urban sector of the Thai economy. Therefore, such investment can be described as having made positive contributions to the short-term growth of the economy during the 1960s and early 1970s. However, the industrialization process and the resulting economic performance have been less than impressive when compared with such countries as Korea, Singapore, Taiwan, or even Malaysia. In fact, many would consider Thailand's industrialization program a failure from the long-term overall economic development point of view because the industries that have come into existence during the past decade or so are by and large capital-intensive, urban-based and catering mainly to urban markets. This pattern of industrialization has resulted in increasing disparities between the rich and the poor, and between the urban and the rural sectors. Foreign investments and investors are considered to have contributed to this unhealthy pattern of economic growth, and have become a target for attack from the vocal public. It is in this context and perspective that the recent sudden upsurge of social and political unrest in the traditionally docile Thai society should be interpreted.

The fact of the matter is that despite the disadvantages and harmful effects of foreign investment, it is unlikely that Thailand will change her basic economic policy and reject future foreign investment. In view of the country's economic structure and resource endowments, it would not be in her interest to do so. But in order to minimize the harmful effects of foreign investments that have been experienced in the past, the administrative system must be overhauled.

Indeed, the success or failure of the entire development effort crucially depends on whether Thailand can replace the existing archaic administrative system with a reasonably efficient one. A noted development scholar has aptly pointed out that if a society changes more rapidly than its political (or administrative) system, national development in all fields slows down until the government catches up.

The tables that were used to support the analysis and conclusions of the Sura and Twatchai paper are presented on the following pages.

**Table 5-16**
**Direct Foreign Investment in Thailand, 1965-1972 (Million Baht)**

| | Capital Flow | | | Services Flow | | | | | |
|---|---|---|---|---|---|---|---|---|---|
| Year | Equity | Loans | Interest | Dividends | Profits | Wages | Management Fees | Copyright and Patent Payments | Total |
| *Inflow* | | | | | | | | | |
| 1965 | 860.3 | 50.0 | 7.4 | 1.0 | 10.5 | 4.0 | – | – | 933.2 |
| 1966 | 537.9 | 91.1 | 10.9 | 2.7 | 14.8 | 8.4 | – | – | 665.8 |
| 1967 | 759.2 | 210.1 | 13.3 | 1.1 | 11.6 | 19.4 | – | – | 1,014.7 |
| 1968 | 1,031.5 | 288.5 | 18.5 | 0.8 | 7.7 | 35.0 | – | – | 1,382.0 |
| 1969 | 903.8 | 262.0 | 39.5 | 2.6 | 27.2 | 29.9 | – | – | 1,265.0 |
| 1970 | 675.6 | 328.8 | 58.9 | 2.2 | 38.9 | 7.8 | – | 0.1 | 1,112.3 |
| 1971 | 783.2 | 234.7 | 38.0 | 2.3 | 59.1 | 1.5 | – | 2.1 | 1,120.9 |
| 1972 | 1,165.7 | 388.2 | 32.6 | 6.5 | 69.6 | 2.1 | – | 10.5 | 1,675.2 |
| Total | 6,717.2 | 1,853.4 | 219.1 | 19.2 | 239.4 | 108.1 | – | 12.7 | 9,169.1 |
| *Outflow* | | | | | | | | | |
| 1965 | 12.0 | 28.0 | 189.1 | 34.6 | 169.6 | 8.4 | 14.5 | 26.4 | 482.6 |
| 1966 | 44.5 | 13.9 | 163.6 | 59.6 | 280.4 | 14.7 | 23.9 | 38.7 | 639.3 |
| 1967 | 43.7 | 31.2 | 200.2 | 80.6 | 293.0 | 26.4 | 40.9 | 39.7 | 755.7 |
| 1968 | 11.8 | 68.5 | 247.4 | 123.9 | 209.3 | 48.5 | 24.8 | 49.6 | 783.8 |
| 1969 | 12.6 | 95.7 | 276.9 | 140.6 | 375.9 | 28.7 | 35.7 | 60.8 | 1,026.9 |
| 1970 | 23.7 | 99.9 | 378.2 | 170.9 | 404.9 | 26.1 | 52.8 | 66.2 | 1,222.7 |
| 1971 | 101.0 | 118.3 | 477.6 | 200.9 | 383.7 | 29.5 | 45.0 | 99.9 | 1,455.9 |
| 1972 | 11.0 | 115.8 | 510.1 | 205.8 | 355.5 | 30.0 | 43.6 | 130.9 | 1,402.7 |
| Total | 206.3 | 571.3 | 2,443.1 | 1,016.9 | 2,472.3 | 212.3 | 281.2 | 512.2 | 7,769.6 |

**Table 5-16** (cont.)

*Net Flow*

| | | | | | | | | | |
|---|---|---|---|---|---|---|---|---|---|
| 1965 | 848.3 | 22.0 | −181.7 | −33.6 | −159.1 | −4.4 | −14.5 | −26.4 | 450.6 |
| 1966 | 493.4 | 77.2 | −152.7 | −56.9 | −265.6 | −6.3 | −23.9 | −38.7 | 26.5 |
| 1967 | 715.5 | 178.9 | −186.9 | −79.5 | −281.4 | −7.0 | −40.9 | −39.7 | 259.0 |
| 1968 | 1,019.7 | 220.0 | −228.9 | −123.1 | −201.6 | −13.5 | −24.8 | −49.6 | 598.2 |
| 1969 | 891.2 | 166.3 | −237.4 | −138.0 | −348.7 | 1.2 | −35.7 | −60.8 | 238.1 |
| 1970 | 651.9 | 228.9 | −319.3 | −168.7 | −366.0 | −18.3 | −52.8 | −66.1 | −110.4 |
| 1971 | 682.2 | 116.4 | −439.6 | −198.6 | −324.6 | −28.0 | −45.0 | −97.8 | −335.0 |
| 1972 | 1,154.7 | 272.4 | −477.5 | −199.3 | −285.9 | −27.9 | −43.6 | −120.4 | 272.5 |
| Total | 6,456.9 | 1,282.1 | −2,224.0 | −997.7 | −2,232.9 | −104.2 | −281.2 | −499.5 | 1,399.5 |

Source: Bank of Thailand.

**Table 5-17**
**Comparison of Direct Foreign Investment and Trade Balance, 1965-1972**

| Year | Direct Foreign Investment | Trade Balance | Direct Foreign Investment as % of Trade Balance |
|---|---|---|---|
| 1965 | 870 | –2,492 | 34.9 |
| 1966 | 570 | –4,405 | 12.9 |
| 1967 | 895 | –8,022 | 11.2 |
| 1968 | 1,240 | –10,424 | 11.9 |
| 1969 | 1,057 | –11,244 | 9.4 |
| 1970 | 881 | –12,237 | 7.2 |
| 1971 | 798 | –9,513 | 8.4 |
| 1972 | 1,427 | –8,384 | 17.0 |

Source: Bank of Thailand.

**Table 5-18**
**Investment and Employment in Promoted Enterprises, 1960-1973**

| | Promoted Firms | Total Investment (Million Baht) | Machinery and Equipment (Million Baht) | Estimated Thai Employees (Persons) |
|---|---|---|---|---|
| 1960-62 | 64 | 2,593 | 1,460 | 30,590 |
| 1963-65 | 131 | 3,847 | 2,151 | 26,380 |
| 1966 | 29 | 1,715 | 1,034 | 4,447 |
| 1967 | 76 | 4,436 | 2,510 | 10,780 |
| 1968 | 82 | 2,562 | 1,306 | 10,605 |
| 1969 | 51 | 4,162 | 2,557 | 8,092 |
| 1970 | 54 | 2,726 | 1,512 | 16,590 |
| 1971 | 49 | 770 | 442 | 12,057 |
| 1972 | 61 | 4,079 | 2,444 | 19,719 |
| 1973 | 97 | 7,765 | 2,487 | 21,640 |

Source: Board of Investment.

**Table 5-19**
**Composition of Foreign and Indigenous Equity in Promoted Enterprises, 1960-1973**

| | Promoted Firms | | | | Registered Capital | | |
|---|---|---|---|---|---|---|---|
| | Total Number | Thai (%) | Foreign (%) | Joint (%) | Total M. Baht | Thai (%) | Foreign (%) |
| 1960-69 | 64 | 45.3 | 1.6 | 53.1 | 994 | 75.1 | 24.9 |
| 1963-65 | 131 | 35.9 | 0.8 | 63.3 | 1,274 | 60.7 | 39.3 |
| 1966 | 29 | 41.4 | 6.9 | 51.7 | 512 | 62.9 | 37.1 |
| 1967 | 76 | 46.1 | 3.9 | 50.0 | 952 | 74.1 | 25.9 |
| 1968 | 82 | 46.3 | 9.8 | 43.9 | 615 | 54.7 | 45.3 |
| 1969 | 51 | 47.1 | 1.9 | 51.0 | 1,251 | 64.4 | 35.6 |
| 1970 | 54 | 40.7 | 3.7 | 55.6 | 902 | 68.2 | 31.8 |
| 1971 | 49 | 59.2 | – | 40.8 | 456 | 70.2 | 29.8 |
| 1972 | 61 | 54.1 | – | 45.9 | 1,008 | 76.6 | 23.4 |
| 1973 | 97 | 48.5 | 1.0 | 50.5 | 1,284 | 77.0 | 23.0 |

Source: Board of Investment.

**Table 5-20**
**Ownership of Equity by Nationality, 1960-1973**

| Ownership of Registered Capital | | |
|---|---|---|
| Nationality | Million Baht | (%) |
| Thai | 6,474 | 69.2 |
| Japanese | 1,074 | 11.5 |
| American | 467 | 5.0 |
| Taiwanese | 446 | 4.8 |
| European | 336 | 3.6 |
| Others | 555 | 5.9 |
| Total | 9,352 | 100.0 |

Source: Board of Investment.

**Table 5-21**
**Equity Participation by Nationality by Industry Group, 1960-1973 (Percentage)**

| Industry Group | Thai | Japanese | American | Others |
|---|---|---|---|---|
| Agriculture Products & Fishery | 65.1 | 5.6 | 23.2 | 6.1 |
| Metal, Metal Products & Mineral Products | 64.3 | 6.8 | 12.8 | 16.1 |
| Food and Cold Storage | 74.0 | 5.7 | 4.1 | 16.2 |
| Textile & Fiber Products | 65.5 | 20.5 | 1.2 | 12.8 |
| Wood Products | 84.2 | 2.1 | 8.5 | 5.2 |
| Chemical & Chemical Products | 61.6 | 17.9 | 2.7 | 17.8 |
| Petroleum & Petro-chemical Products | 43.4 | 8.8 | 19.5 | 28.3 |
| Rubber Products, Plastic Products | 57.2 | 9.1 | 13.6 | 20.1 |
| Electrical Appliances & Accessories | 56.7 | 9.1 | 17.7 | 16.5 |
| Labor Saving Devices, Engines, etc. | 76.5 | 3.4 | 7.1 | 13.0 |
| Rock, Clay, Ceramic, Lime & Cement | 81.4 | 1.5 | 5.6 | 11.5 |
| Glass Sheet, Spectacle, Glass | 66.6 | 15.4 | – | 18.0 |
| Paints | 39.5 | 6.2 | 12.9 | 41.4 |
| Vehicle, Spare Parts | 59.2 | 29.6 | 5.2 | 6.0 |
| Hotels | 71.8 | 1.5 | 12.6 | 14.1 |
| Trans and Others | 69.4 | 6.4 | 3.8 | 20.4 |
| Total | 66.9 | 9.5 | 8.9 | 14.7 |

Source: Board of Investment.

**Table 5-22**
**Location of Promoted Factories in Operation, 1960-1973**

| Region | Number of Factories | (%) |
|---|---|---|
| Central Region | | |
| Bangkok Metropolis and Samutprakarn | 308 | 57.9 |
| Other Provinces in the Central Region | 151 | 28.4 |
| Northern Region | 26 | 4.9 |
| North-Eastern Region | 18 | 3.4 |
| Southern Region | 29 | 5.4 |
| Total | 532 | 100.0 |

Source: Board of Investment.

**Table 5-23**
**Distribution of Promoted Enterprises by Industrial Group, 1960-1973**

| Industry | Promoted Projects[a] | | Reg'd Capital | |
|---|---|---|---|---|
| | Number | (%) | M. Baht | (%) |
| 1. Agriculture Products & Fishery | 28 | 4.1 | 455 | 4.3 |
| 2. Metal, Metal Products & Mineral Products | 80 | 11.8 | 1,714 | 16.3 |
| 3. Food and Cold Storage | 87 | 12.8 | 1,013 | 9.7 |
| 4. Textile & Fiber Products | 128 | 18.8 | 2,201 | 20.9 |
| 5. Wood Products | 47 | 6.9 | 492 | 4.7 |
| 6. Chemical & Chemical Products | 16 | 2.3 | 235 | 2.2 |
| 7. Petroleum & Petro-chemical Products | 10 | 1.5 | 600 | 5.7 |
| 8. Rubber Products, Plastic Products | 39 | 5.7 | 509 | 4.9 |
| 9. Electrical Appliances & Accessories | 45 | 6.6 | 385 | 3.7 |
| 10. Labor Saving Devices, Engines, et. | 27 | 4.0 | 545 | 5.2 |
| 11. Rock, Clay, Ceramic, Lime & Cement | 29 | 4.3 | 780 | 7.4 |
| 12. Glass Sheet, Spectacle, Glass | 5 | 0.7 | 39 | 0.4 |
| 13. Paints | 11 | 1.6 | 78 | 0.7 |
| 14. Vehicle, Spare Parts | 42 | 6.2 | 335 | 3.2 |
| 15. Hotels | 59 | 8.7 | 943 | 9.0 |
| 16. Transportation and Others | 27 | 4.0 | 178 | 1.7 |
| All Industries | 680 | 100.0 | 10,502 | 100.0 |

[a]1960-1971 only.
Source: Board of Investment.

**Table 5-24**
**Japanese Equity Participation in Thai Enterprises, 1968-1972**

| Year | All Industries | Textiles | Automobiles | Iron & Steel | Food | Others |
|---|---|---|---|---|---|---|
| Paid up Capital (Million Baht) | | | | | | |
| 1968 | 649 | 247 | 167 | 92 | 69 | 74 |
| 1969 | 957 | 520 | 176 | 92 | 69 | 100 |
| 1970 | 1,157 | 681 | 176 | 92 | 84 | 124 |
| 1971 | 1,212 | 706 | 166 | 99 | 84 | 157 |
| 1972 | 1,543 | 856 | 183 | 158 | 133 | 213 |
| Japanese Participation (%) | | | | | | |
| 1968 | 73 | 76 | 73 | 62 | 91 | 62 |
| 1969 | 71 | 72 | 71 | 62 | 91 | 60 |
| 1970 | 68 | 68 | 70 | 62 | 88 | 58 |
| 1971 | 67 | 67 | 71 | 60 | 88 | 55 |
| 1972 | 59 | 56 | 71 | 55 | 73 | 50 |

Source: Japanese Chamber of Commerce.

**Table 5-25**
**Sources of Raw Materials Used by Japanese Investment in Thailand,[a] 1968-1972**

| | Total Raw Material Value | Local Sources | Japan | Other Sources |
|---|---|---|---|---|
| | Million Baht | Percentage of Total Value | | |
| Total | | | | |
| 1968 | 1,651 | 20.8 | 67.8 | 11.4 |
| 1969 | 1,911 | 20.3 | 70.1 | 9.6 |
| 1970 | 2,368 | 24.4 | 60.8 | 14.8 |
| 1971 | 2,793 | 27.3 | 57.7 | 15.0 |
| 1972 | 3,415 | 34.1 | 54.1 | 11.8 |
| Textiles | | | | |
| 1968 | 355 | 41.0 | 31.9 | 27.1 |
| 1969 | 351 | 40.8 | 44.4 | 14.8 |
| 1970 | 652 | 39.4 | 30.0 | 30.6 |
| 1971 | 820 | 38.9 | 34.2 | 26.9 |
| 1972 | 960 | 45.6 | 38.9 | 15.5 |
| Automobiles | | | | |
| 1968 | 631 | 12.1 | 87.2 | 0.7 |
| 1969 | 826 | 12.0 | 87.3 | 0.7 |
| 1970 | 736 | 12.1 | 86.8 | 1.1 |
| 1971 | 886 | 15.9 | 82.5 | 1.6 |
| 1972 | 1,073 | 16.0 | 83.0 | 0.9 |
| Iron & Steel | | | | |
| 1968 | 483 | 7.2 | 75.7 | 17.1 |
| 1969 | 526 | 8.3 | 69.7 | 22.0 |
| 1970 | 646 | 11.0 | 68.4 | 20.6 |
| 1971 | 713 | 16.5 | 62.5 | 21.0 |
| 1972 | 736 | 24.0 | 52.4 | 23.5 |
| Food | | | | |
| 1968 | 76 | 80.2 | 19.8 | – |
| 1969 | 87 | 93.1 | 6.9 | – |
| 1970 | 112 | 89.1 | 10.9 | – |
| 1971 | 134 | 94.2 | 5.2 | 0.6 |
| 1972 | 222 | 97.3 | 2.2 | 0.5 |

| | | | | |
|---|---|---|---|---|
| Others | | | | |
| 1968 | 106 | 23.7 | 70.6 | 5.7 |
| 1969 | 120 | 18.1 | 75.7 | 0.2 |
| 1970 | 222 | 27.7 | 69.0 | 3.3 |
| 1971 | 240 | 24.1 | 62.2 | 13.7 |
| 1972 | 424 | 38.0 | 45.5 | 16.5 |

[a]Including joint ventures

Source: Japanese Chamber of Commerce.

## Discussion: The Sura and Twatchai Paper

Sura began by noting that while the paper he and Twatchai had prepared confined itself to a study of direct private investment, he intended to discuss it in the broader context of the Seminar. Direct investment, he pointed out, reflects foreign aid policies since much of it is guaranteed by the government of the investor's home country or is given some less direct form of public support. Also, the Thai government grants special privileges to foreign investments in areas it wishes to promote. Yet the grant element in such assistance, from the point of view of the host country, is likely to be very small or negative. That is, virtually all the benefit might go to the foreign investor as reflected in his profits.

The foreign investor's profit motive ought to be clearly recognized and candidly acknowledged by both sides, since foreign investors often claim that they will be making great contributions to Thailand's economic development, and Thais may be misled into thinking that the foreigner's motives are altruistic. Most foreign investment is in the form of joint ventures with Thai partners, but even though capital participation by foreigners may be minor, their influence in positions of management is often dominant, leading to the criticism that the transfer of managerial know-how and technical information may be unduly restrained.

Private investment, in Sura's opinion, is more attractive than aid in at least one respect, since Thailand keeps full autonomy in control of the former. Further, foreign investment is less likely than governmental aid to be distorted by political bias, and it is more likely to stimulate domestic entrepreneurship. Thus the question becomes how to attract foreign investment and at the same time improve its quality.

Turning the matter around, Sura also noted that direct grants-in-aid from foreign governments might be given to organizations in the Thai private sector, such as trade associations or the Chamber of Commerce. Business organizations such as these have been weak in Thailand but might play useful roles if they could be strengthened.

In the discussion, Japanese investment was singled out for particular attention. It was pointed out that Japanese investment amounts to about 40 percent of total foreign investment in Thailand even though senior public officials in Japan regard 30 percent as a tolerable limit within any one country. The problem is heightened by the fact that Thailand's industrial promotion policy coincides in time with a Japanese decision to expand direct investment abroad. It may be harder for Thais to accept different modes of behavior by Japanese than has been the case with Westerners, since the Japanese are Asians and are therefore expected to be more likely to conform to local customs, manners, and forms of courtesy. The Japanese were criticized for having only economic rather than social contacts with Thais in Thailand, for not sharing control with Thais or appointing them to high managerial positions, for selling inferior goods in Thailand as opposed to Japan itself and Western markets, and for exporting "dirty" industries rather than adding to the pollution of Japan itself. But one participant contended that other foreign businessmen, particularly American, deserved and were receiving similar criticism. In response to some of these criticisms, Mr. Wakabayashi pointed out that Japanese investment came to Thailand only in accord with Thai policy. Much of the criticism, he felt, was emotional. The language barrier between Thai and Japanese posed great problems in raising Thai staff members to high positions in Japanese firms. The point was also made that Thai schools and universities can contribute to reductions in the language barrier by greater interest in instruction in Japanese language and culture. It was suggested that Japanese are subject to special criticism because Japan is the largest foreign investor in Thailand. It was pointed out that the Japanese, to their credit, are not as involved in the domestic politics of Thailand as are some other foreigners.

Puey asked how high a priority Thailand should give to foreign investment in industry. He regards industrial promotion as being of far less importance than rural development, political and social reform, and development of education and health. Foreign investment, he stated, should be promoted to some extent; but it will affect only a small minority of the people. Much more attention must be paid to the goals of industrial promotion. He believes that promotion policies, such as that giving promotional privileges to investment in hotels, must be changed. The government should give concessions, such as subsidization of electric power, to firms locating in outlying districts. Agribusiness development should be given high priority.

But industrial promotion and foreign investment cannot be considered in isolation. The crucial question is the complexion of the government. There must be, according to Puey, speculation both on what ought to be done and what it is realistic to think can be done by 1980. The concentration of wealth and power in the hands of a few families must be corrected. Thai banks are pervasively involved in industrialization, and this is widely resented. Labor unrest poses grave problems. Wages must go up. And so labor costs will go up. How can this unrest be dealt with without violence?

Suppose, Puey suggested, Thailand moves toward a form of democratic socialism, with high and progressive taxes, and with labor participation both in management and on boards of directors. Financial institutions encouraging stock purchases by small investors, including workers buying equity stock in their companies through payroll deduction plans, might also be developed. Thais must start thinking along unfamiliar lines such as these, he urged, and in general about individual and social justice to avoid labor unrest and to create a society where labor and capital can cooperate in basic harmony even while quarreling from time to time.

Concern was expressed that Sura and Twatchai's data suggested that the rate of capital outflow has been accelerating in recent years (c.f. Table 5-16), becoming a force worsening Thailand's balance of payments. Investment promotion may have led to a bias in favor of capital-intensive enterprises as their data (Table 5-18) also show that investment per worker is very high in the promoted industries.

Problems were noted growing out of the fact that most of the Thai partners in firms with foreign participation come from a small wealthy group which is not likely to have a great deal of concern for social developmental objectives, such as transfer of technology, full employment, income redistribution, and decentralization of industry into regions outside the metropolitan area. Nothing would be gained in terms of these social objectives by ultimate transfer of ownership and control from foreigners to such domestic elements, in the opinion of one participant, who then went on to add that indeed the Thai people as a whole had very little to gain from direct foreign investment and the less of it Thailand had, the better.

There were other criticisms of foreign investors and their behavior. It was claimed that foreign businessmen are encouraging corruption among government officials as well as becoming equally culpable themselves through payment of bribes. In one participant's opinion foreign firms should be doing more to facilitate transfer of knowledge through one-the-job technical training of their employees. But it was also argued that the level of morality and business ethics of Thai and foreign businessmen are pretty much the same, and concern about foreigners' conduct is no justification for business regulations which do not treat both groups equally.

Other topics discussed included the need for coordination among various governmental agencies in developing a consistent set of policies and practices in dealing with foreign investors, and a summary by Snoh of efforts by NESDB to achieve such coordination; the importance of agribusiness enterprises in developing labor-intensive methods as well as in dispersing industrial employment spatially; and changes in U.S. aid policy mandating greater attention from AID to problems of low-income people, rural development, and benefit to people who had not benefited from earlier AID programs, all of which were regarded by the speaker as being fully in accord with the previously expressed opinion that industrial promotion should be given a rather low priority in Thailand's development plans.

# 6 A Summing Up

In opening the Seminar and welcoming the participants on behalf of the sponsoring institutions, Dr. Vinyu Vichit-Vadakan defined the basic theme as discussion and analysis of the problems involved in foreign aid and other forms of financial assistance to Thailand in a period in which very major social, political, and economic changes, already underway, would be taking place. The Chairman then urged the Seminar to look at these problems as interconnected by three links: Thailand's needs; the institutional framework within which aid will be received and used; and the motivations and conduct of donors. By the time the last paper had been presented and discussed, it was clear that there were several and not always entirely harmonious variations on the basic theme, and that no consensus had emerged as to the strength of the three links or how they interlocked. But if uniformity of opinion and sets of specific policy prescriptions for both Thais and donors did not emerge, nevertheless a great deal of light was shed on very fundamental and perplexing questions. Thus there were no Seminar resolutions or recommendations debated in the final session; instead, the bulk of that session was devoted to observations on the Seminar as a whole by three participants whose backgrounds, experience, and current positions gave to each a significant and distinctive perspective on the issues—Ernst, Puey, and Snoh.

Ernst spoke of each of the three links—needs, domestic institutions, and donors' concerns—in turn. Beginning with Thailand's needs for assistance in achieving its national goals for development, he noted that these goals need to be agreed upon and articulated, for without such an articulation proposals for specific projects and programs have little meaning. These goals will have to be creative and imaginative to attract donors in the future.

Productivity boosts and resource mobilization are essential, Ernst continued. Donors will demand evidence of serious domestic efforts to reallocate resources, implying major reforms in such areas as taxation and delivery of aid benefits to the people. An important problem in Thailand, he continued, is underutilization of existing human talents in areas of social importance, such as education and health care. Effective delivery systems are essential. For example, aid has been given to extension services for agricultural development for many years, and large numbers of Thais have been given excellent training, both in Thailand and abroad, in agricultural sciences. But the extension service has failed to get the results of all of this applied on the nation's farms. The remedy does not lie in more aid, but in correction by the Thai government of inadequacies in the agencies responsible for the existing extension programs.

Turning to redistribution of rewards, Ernst questioned whether the present economic system in Thailand is such that people are rewarded for their contributions to national development in terms of such things as monetary or price rewards and availability of services.

Almost nothing that can be done by 1980, he noted, can prevent Thailand's population from rising to roughly 100 million by the year 2000. But the "hero" of 2000 might be the unborn Thai, if proper policies are established and implemented now.

In Ernst's opinion, efforts to achieve democracy, to the extent that they are successful, may be important in resource development since stronger and more autonomous local government will permit projects to be formulated and managed at the local level and will allow for small-scale test, experiment, and evaluation. Thailand's economic and political systems are growing in independence and maturity, and so the nation is entering into new relations with donors. Thailand ought not be primarily dependent on one donor any longer, but should be enlarging her own choices. And on their side, donors must be considering alternative choices for use of aid funds–including other countries.

In discussing domestic institutions and mechanisms, Ernst mentioned that efficient planning, coordinating, and budgetary processes are very important. Thus the roles of NESDB, DTEC, and the Bureau of the Budget are vital ones. Further, to have projects function effectively when they are supported by foreign aid but carried out by Thais, the Civil Service Commission must be conscientious in allocating and assigning appropriate Thai personnel to such projects and supporting activities. It is obviously crucial that intermediate organizations which execute projects and transmit the aid, such as the Bank for Agriculture and Agricultural Cooperatives, Scientific Research Institute, and the Industrial Finance Corporation of Thailand, be efficient. Finally, strong and capable organs of local government can contribute much to the success of projects in their areas.

Turning to donor concerns and constraints, Ernst noted that the 25 least-developed nations, "the poorest of the poor," will get higher priority in the future from both the multilateral donors and the U.S., especially in aid programs of a highly concessionary nature. Further, concessionality must be justified in terms of the local efforts both to raise resources for public purposes and then to allocate these resources to development. In this connection, it is significant and disappointing that the Thai development budget has stagnated over recent years. Where, he asked, is evidence of domestic effort? In regard to results, he asked whether Thailand was using aid correctly. The present portfolio of U.S. aid projects to Thailand is, he reported, now a matter of some concern. These projects are not, in the main, directed to solution of the tough problems of social justice and equity in development. Donors must be worried about how long aid will go on, when it will end, and under what conditions. This concern for terminality holds for specific projects and programs which may drag on for years after the need for foreign guidance and participation has ended, and also for the aid commitment to a specific country. Finally, he noted once again that U.S. policy was shifting from a political rationale for assistance to Thailand to a new, developmental rationale. This would be, he hoped, supportive of Thailand's stated concerns for new forms of social and economic development.

Puey, following up on the points made by Ernst, stated that in his estimation Thailand's greatest weakness lies in determination of national goals. In Thailand there is a great deal of concern with details of development, but no effort to integrate the details into a coherent set of national goals and objectives. One reason is that all of the important agencies which Ernst had called attention to are very large and virtually empires unto themselves. There is no coordination. And thus development planning is out of focus and blurred. The World Bank made this criticism several years ago, but there has been no real change. Indeed, all of the old obstacles to coordination are still there and new ones are growing. The failure to coordinate extends beyond formulation and administration of developmental efforts. It is endemic to Thailand. In the Thai Parliament, for example, there has been discussion of needed reforms in the system of justice, from police through the prisons; but the administration of justice seems to be getting worse. And problems are growing in labor and industry. When one turns to public administration, one finds no coordination but rather several departments doing the same things—or else no organization doing things that should be done. To avoid Amara's "nightmare" scenario in 1980, reform of the system must begin now. No organization, no matter how powerful or well established, should be taken for granted. The agencies that are not doing their jobs should be abolished. Thais in high positions of influence and leadership must look at needs and solutions with clear minds, which the "mandarins" of the Civil Service themselves cannot do. And foreign aid cannot help in this process. In the past, foreign assistance was useful in establishing reforms in accounting and budgeting, but Thai public agencies are well past that stage and further reform must be internal. Foreign aid should be used, if Thailand must have it between now and 1980, for more productive purposes.

Puey closed his remarks by expressing his agreement with Ernst and other participants on the importance of recognizing the needs of countries which are poorer than Thailand. Thailand will not be strong, he pointed out, as long as neighbors such as Laos are poor and weak.

Sakda elaborated on Ernst's and Puey's observations on determination of national goals by commenting that a crucial problem was that the top civil servants and others high in the national government, rightly designated as the "mandarins" by Puey, might exclude organizations and representatives of labor, agriculture, other commerce and industry, and local government—among others—from any participation in determining goals and priorities and in defining social responsibility.

Snoh then offered his overall impressions of the Seminar. He thought that the

Seminar had made a genuine step forward in ways of thinking about aid from both Thai and donor points of view. Thais may have been overly influenced and indiscriminate in their reactions to offers of aid by the lure of getting something for nothing. Donors were certainly very much influenced by their own interests, political objectives, and–perhaps most important–ideologies. Even the multilateral donors pressed their own views regarding developmental means and priorities on Thailand. An interaction between the attitude of taking anything if it were free and donors' preoccupations with their own objectives has in part led to the present unsatisfactory state of reality revealed at the Seminar. But during the Seminar sessions, participants from both sides had reflected an objective, systematic approach that all could work with. It was clear all around that the primary responsibility lies with Thailand and that foreign aid can play only a minor role. Snoh observed that Puey himself had expressed the nation's goals eloquently and that Thailand needed eloquence. If the eloquence, wisdom, and experience of men like Puey can energize the younger generation of functionaries, the system will succeed. The functionaries must be energized from oustide because they are "mandarins," complacent virtually by definition. Indeed, only the "mandarins" can afford to work for the Thai government.

Cooperative efforts among Thais, Snoh continued, are essential. Puey had mentioned that lawyers were coming together to consider sweeping and integrated reforms throughout the system of justice. Another example would be the group of political scientists who had worked hard and effectively together on a draft constitution. Economists and social thinkers have an as yet unfulfilled responsibility to come together and work cooperatively on the problems of systematic social and economic restructuring. It must be essentially a Thai effort, with but a marginal contribution from foreign aid sources. The marginal contribution could, though, make the difference between success and failure. He did not have to tell economists how important marginal factors could be, Snoh concluded.

One of the participants from a multilateral aid agency pointed out that economic development has not yet solved the basic problems of poverty and misery, although planners and economists have been making grandiose promises for many years. Indeed, solution of these problems may not even have been one of the goals of those in both donor and recipient countries responsible for formulating development strategies. When one looks at poverty, misery, and lack of hope as the basic problems of Thailand, one finds strong support for Puey's view that there is only a small need for foreign aid and a great need for concerted domestic effort.

Amara commented that the phrase "foreign aid" might have been an inappropriate one in the title given to the Seminar. It seemed to him that the more the "aid" given by donor nations, the more they profited from their relations with the recipient countries. Given the ulterior motives of the donors, and recognizing that they had benefited more from their "aid" than had the recipients, Amara proposed "external inputs" as a more apt phrase. He then described, briefly, a benign and optimistic scenario of alternative and future conferences he envisaged himself attending. Perhaps what should be under discussion is how Thailand can free herself from foreign exploitation or, very bluntly, how the nation must resist economic imperialism. He saw the answer traced out in the titles of a set of additional conferences. First, and at the present time, there should be a conference on "Mobilizing Thailand's Resources." In the future, and in recognition of the fact that no nation can develop without an interchange of ideas and technology, he hoped for a conference on "International Exchange." And before the year 2000 he would like to take part in a conference on "Thailand's Direct and Indirect Contributions to the Earlier Developed Countries."

One could draw a very negative conclusion from portions of the Seminar papers and discussion. In terms of the criterion by which financial aid is usually dispersed, a strong case can be made for terminating all foreign aid to Thailand under present circumstances. There are several considerations pointing to this conclusion from the points of view of various donors. The direct and ulterior interests of the U.S. in Thailand are being reduced as the U.S. disengages from Southeast Asia in a military sense and seeks detente with both the Soviet Union and the Peoples' Republic of China. Japan's commercial interests do not seem to have been furthered by her aid efforts. Rather, it is more likely that Japan's economic objectives in Thailand will be better served by improvements in the relations between the Japanese and Thai business communities and by the development of strong and mutually beneficial trade relations. There are grave doubts that Thailand has the institutional capabilities to make effective use of genuinely developmental aid. And if one accepts at face value the commitment of both developed countries and the multilateral donors to redirect aid to those in most need of it, Thailand's claim must rank lower than those of many poorer nations.

The Seminar also brought out reasons why, from Thailand's own point of view, the case for continued aid is an uneasy one. The nation's developmental goals for the 1970s and 1980s are far more complex than those for the 1950s and 1960s, and the evidence from those earlier years is that foreign assistance is most effective in projects with simple, noncontroversial objectives and straightforward technical solutions. It is doubtful if foreign assistance, particularly in the form of advisors, can be of much real help as the nation's efforts shift from aggregate economic growth to more of a concern with social and economic justice and a redress of imbalances that aid since World War II may have helped aggravate. There is a growing concern about the competence of foreign advisors compared to that of educated and often underutilized Thais, and a growing awareness that advisors' services are not free of support costs to Thailand. Thailand's international posture will very likely shift toward neutrality, perhaps within a regional bloc, making the solicitation of aid from particular national donors fraught with political complications. And finally, virtually all of the participants at the Seminar would share Puey's view that one of the nation's most important development objectives should be self-reliance (as distinguished from an impossible quest for self-sufficiency) and an end to all aid but loans made available by international institutions which Thailand has helped to create and continues to support.

Yet the conclusion that future foreign aid to Thailand is unwarranted is not a tenable one to draw from careful consideration of the Seminar proceedings. While Thailand is far from being among the "poorest of the poor," Amara's harsh scenario for the 1980s and the virtual certainty that there will be approximately 100 million Thais in the year 2000 both point to the inescapable fact that new initiatives in development are essential. The contribution of foreign aid to such new approaches and efforts will be small, as will be the magnitude of the aid needed; but in light of several compelling observations that the small contributions could be crucial ones it would seem utterly irresponsible to contend that there is no need for further aid to Thailand. Just as Thailand cannot live easily in a world where many still poorer nations are racked with misery and despair, so the wealthy developed nations have a very real stake in seeing to it that 100 million Thais in the year 2000 have escaped from the poverty and injustice that now appears to be one quite likely fate.

Despite the overt criterion of immediate need, in terms of which Thailand's case for assistance does not appear strong, rationality dictates that donors give heavy weight to the overall productivity of the action in which they are engaged. Furtherance of even purely humanitarian goals requires that a high priority be assigned by donors to countries where such aid can, in the long run, make a difference. Aid to Thailand may prove crucial in preventing the Amara scenario from becoming reality and in helping Thailand to join the ranks of the more highly developed nations. By allocating support in a long-run as well as a short-run context, donors might well further their own goals most effectively.

Barbara Ward, as cited by Supachai, noted that a major obstacle to future foreign aid is a growing sense that it has failed. But she made this point as one step in an argument that this obstacle must be overcome because generous and intelligently conceived aid is essential, indeed a last hope, for development and economic progress in many of the nations of the world. As has been said of Christianity, the only trouble with genuinely developmental foreign aid may be that it has never been truly and wholeheartedly tried.

# 7 Conclusions

It is an oversimplification and yet of the essence to say that Thailand's economic future may well depend on the result of two opposing forces—the rate of growth of food production and the rate of population growth. A rate of natural increase of approximately 3.2 percent per year in recent decades has already created a population pattern that is likely to cause the Thai population to grow from its present level of approximately forty million to around a hundred million by the year 2000. Clearly, the precarious balance between food and people poses a dire threat to the very viability of an economy based largely on the exportation of food. Put bluntly, Thailand may have to consume what would otherwise be its exports.

Despite Amara's scenario and the discussion which it engendered, most of the participants did not view Thailand's future in such simple and stark terms. If they had, the focus of the papers and the discussion would have been almost exclusively upon financial aid as it relates to agricultural productivity and to population control. Though history may indicate the appropriateness of such a narrow view, the present volume gains much in interest because of the very large range of developmental concerns which it recounts—from how to determine the degree of labor intensity that should characterize road construction techniques in a developing Thailand to the type of political interrelationships that may exist between the nations of this region in the 1980s. The papers and discussion thus provide a comprehensive view of many of the complexities of the developmental process in Thailand.

Any view that encompasses a part of the future must depend for its validity upon knowledge of the present. And in no country do the economists fully understand the structure and operation of even that part of the economy which captures their primary interest. Economists view but the tip of an iceberg. The great mass of economic actions, decisions, and interrelationships occurs and exists beyond their surveillance. Thus it is that a partial glimpse of the same reality can give birth to the disparate views of a Milton Friedman and a Paul Sweezy.

Hence we could wish for a better and more direct grasp of the reality that is the Thai economy. What is actually occurring now, particularly in the private sector? How quickly is industrialization occurring? How rapidly are markets growing and adding to the interdependence of the economy? How competitive are the various industries within the private sector? What can one expect from concentrations of economic power such as the banks, the rice export cartel, or the "private" enterprises such as cement and sugar? What is the rate of private capital formation? What are some of the more important technological developments now occurring in Thai industry, commerce, and agriculture? A host of unanswered questions plague us, hovering at our elbow and by their continued presence reminding us that, in relating financial aid to Thai economic and social development, we are hampered by the limitations of our knowledge of the present reality.

Nonetheless, man must not meekly bow to the fates simply because their features are only vaguely discernible. The concern and intellectual vigor shown by the participants at the Chieng Mai Seminar are ample evidence that Thais such as these have no intention of doing so. They and a growing number of others like them will work to achieve not only a higher level of material rewards, but also a nation characterized by greater social, political, and economic equity. The goals are admirable, as befits the people, and the U.S. and the world in general have a stake in their attainment.

The case for financial aid to Thailand, as noted elsewhere herein, rests primarily on the overall productivity of such aid. This is a country whose record and potential set it apart as one of the less developed nations with a real chance of joining the ranks of the more highly developed. The fact that the magnitude of financial aid will be small relative to the other variables that will determine the outcome makes it all the more important that such assistance be wisely deployed.

The thorough scrutiny of financial aid to Thailand in the 1980s provided by the papers and discussions which comprise the present volume is replete in its analysis of problems and obstacles with indications of where, and how, financial aid might well be employed to help Thailand achieve its economic and social goals. But the financial aid that is likely to be available to Thailand is of such small magnitude that a priority ranking of the various needs for financial assistance, from a national point of view, is itself badly needed. While agreement on this point was unanimous, the Seminar produced no such priority ranking.

Despite the dictum concerning the territory which angels shun, and hoping that presumptiousness will not preclude serious consideration, we suggest that financial aid to Thailand in the 1980s be sought and granted in terms of priority ranking based on the (admittedly oversimplified) population-food supply relationship with which this concluding section began. Broaden "population" to mean the human resource, including dimensions other than its magnitude; and depart from "food supply" to encompass nonagricultural growth that will reduce the need to export food or which will provide products which Thailand can trade for food from abroad. Further, recognize that both quality of population and "food" in the broadest sense of nourishment involve rural development and social and political as well as economic goals. But keep an eye through time on the basic population-food supply relationship, using the degree of movement away from the miasma which an imbalance in the two describes as an indication of how far it is permissible to depart, in assigning financial aid priorities, from its imperatives. The first priority, after all, is to prevent Amara's scenario from becoming a reality, since all the other social, political, and economic aspirations voiced at the seminar are utterly dependent on success at this most fundamental level.

# Index

# About the Editors

**W. David Maxwell** received the B.A. from the University of North Carolina in 1949 and the Ph.D. from the Johns Hopkins University in 1958. He has taught at the University of South Carolina, Tulane University (where he served as Chairman of the Economics Department), Thammasat University (as a Rockefeller Foundation Visiting Scholar), Indiana University, and Texas A&M University. He has contributed to the professional literature in economics, business administration, and educational administration. Currently Dean of the College of Liberal Arts at Texas A&M, he has served on short-term assignments to Thailand for The Rockefeller Foundation, the Asia Society, and AID.

**W. Lee Baldwin** received the B.A. from Duke University in 1951 and the Ph.D. from Princeton University in 1958. He has served as Chairman of the Social Sciences Division and Chairman of the Economics Department at Dartmouth, Visiting Assistant Professor at Princeton, and as a Brookings Research Professor. From June 1968 to June 1970 and from June 1974 to June 1975 he was a Visiting Professor (sponsored by The Rockefeller Foundation) at Thammasat University in Bangkok. The author of two books and numerous articles in professional journals, he is currently professor of economics at Dartmouth.